LifePrints

ESL FOR ADULTS

SECOND EDITION

3

Christy M. Newman

New Readers Press

LifePrints 3, 2nd Edition
ISBN 978-1-56420-314-4

Copyright © 2002, 1995 New Readers Press
New Readers Press
Division of ProLiteracy Worldwide
1320 Jamesville Avenue, Syracuse, New York 13210
www.newreaderspress.com

Printed in the United States of America
9 8 7 6 5

All proceeds from the sale of New Readers Press materials
support literacy programs in the United States and worldwide.

Developmental Editor: Paula L. Schlusberg
Copy Editor: Judi Lauber
Production Director: Heather Witt
Designers: Fran Forstadt, Shelagh Clancy
Cover Designer: Kimbrly Koennecke
Illustrators: Animotion, Jerry Bates, Dick Falzoi, James P. Wallace
Cover Illustrator: James P. Wallace
Production Specialist: Alexander R. Jones

Series Development: Robert Ventre Associates, Inc.
                        Course Crafters, Inc.

Table of Contents

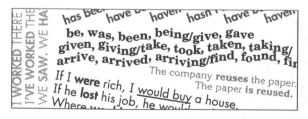

1 2 3 4 5 6 7 8 9 10 11 12
Continuing Education ■ ■ ■ ■ ■ ■

In the Computer Lab

Where are these people?
What do you think they are studying?
How do you feel about using a computer?

Who's in the Lab Today?

Four friends are working in the computer lab today.
**Underline the sentence in each story that tells why
each person is in the lab.**

Diep Tran is a single parent with two young children. She studied science in Vietnam. Now she is working part-time as a laboratory assistant in a hospital. The hospital is getting a new computer system. Diep is taking a computer course so that she'll be prepared to use the new system.

Yolette Jamison is married. She came to the United States from Haiti. She's the assistant manager of an athletic shoe store. She uses a computer to keep track of inventory. She wants to learn more about computers so that she can get an office job.

Stan Wolanski is single and lives with his parents. He and his family came from Poland. Stan works as a gardener. He wants to be his own boss. He's taking business courses so that he can have his own landscaping business someday.

Roberto Silva is married with two children. He and his family came from Puerto Rico. He's a waiter at a hotel restaurant. He works until midnight and only sees his family on weekends. He's studying computers so that he can get a different kind of job.

Yolette brought in a newspaper article about different kinds of adult education programs in the area. Her friends in the computer lab wanted to know more about their different choices.

Adult Education: *What's Available?*

Planning for college and careers can be an exciting time. But it can also be a time of stress and indecision. According to Ronald Briggs, academic advisor at Tri-County Community College, "Many students think that a four-year college is their only choice. They are intimidated by the requirements they think they have to meet. The first thing I do is make sure that adults know what's out there. I always give them a rundown of the main kinds of educational programs available to them."

- **General Educational Development (GED)** is a national high school equivalency program for adults who do not have a high school diploma. Many local adult education programs, school districts, community colleges, and universities offer classes to prepare adults for the GED exam. Classes include work in grammar, writing, math, science, social studies, and literature.

- **Vocational Programs** offer training to prepare students for many kinds of jobs. The subjects include business skills, hairstyling, drafting, air conditioning and refrigeration repair, and auto mechanics.

Vocational training programs are offered by vocational schools, business schools, and many adult education programs.

- **Associate Degree Programs** are two-year programs offered by community colleges, junior colleges, and some business schools. They are useful for adults who need career skills quickly or who are not ready or able to attend four-year colleges. Associate degree credits can be transferred to four-year college programs. Associate degrees are awarded in a wide variety of subjects, including liberal arts, early childhood education, computer technology, health care, and business administration.

Answer the questions.

1. Have you attended any programs like these?
2. What educational programs are you interested in? Why?
3. What programs or subjects might be useful for your goals? Why?

What Classes Should I Take?

A. Complete the story.

Stan needs help deciding which

_____ to take next semester.
　　　　1

He has taken Introduction to _____
　　　　　　　　　　　　　　　　　　2

and Beginning _____ Processing. His counselor, Mr. Briggs, said that
　　　　　　　　3

Basic _____ is a prerequisite for all other _____
　　　　　4　　　　　　　　　　　　　　　　　　　　　　　　　　　5

courses. Prerequisites must be taken _____ other courses.
　　　　　　　　　　　　　　　　　　6

Mr. Briggs also suggested that Stan take a Business _____ class.
　　　　　　　　　　　　　　　　　　　　　　　　　　　　7

Basic Mathematics reviews math for business. It covers addition, subtraction, multiplication, and division of whole numbers; fractions; percents; ratios; and decimals. It uses real business problems. Prerequisite for the business sequence.

Dept.: **Math**　　　　　　　　Cr.: **3**　　　　　Rm.: **202**
Title: **Basic Mathematics**　Instr.: **Moy**　　Time: **8:30–11:30 a.m.**
Course No./Sec.: **85/01**　　Day: **Mon.**

B. Find the abbreviation.

Which abbreviation tells you . . .

	Abbreviation	Meaning
1. the name of the overall subject?		
2. the name of the teacher?		
3. the location of the class?		
4. the units toward graduation that the class fulfills?		

Stan wants to take three classes next term. He works from noon to 6 p.m. every day. Help Stan choose his courses and complete his registration form.

Dept.	No.	Sec.	Course Title	Cr.	Days	Time	Rm.	INSTR.
Math	85	01	**Basic Mathematics**	3	M	8:30–11:30 a.m.	202	Moy
		02			M W	9:30–11:00 a.m.	317	Rogers
		03			T Th	6:00–7:30 p.m.	212	Randall
Engl	125	01	**Business Writing**	3	T Th	2:30–4:00 p.m.	110	Black
		02			M W F	8:00–9:00 a.m.	328	Ross
		03			T	5:00–8:00 p.m.	110	Black
Comp	215	01	**Adv. Word Processing**	2	T	9:30–11:30 a.m.	5	Jordan
		02			F	9:30–11:30 a.m.	5	Jordan

Complete the Registration Form.

ADULT AND CONTINUING EDUCATION

Have you taken an adult education class before?   ☑ Yes   ☐ No

If yes, last course and enrollment date: <u>Intro. to Computers and Beginning Word Processing – Fall '04</u>

SECTION IV

Dept.				No.		Sec.		Course Title	Credits	Office Use Only
M	A	T	H	8	5	0	2		3	

Total number of credits: _____

$80.00 per credit

Amount: _____

Method of Payment:

☐ Cash   ☑ Check or Money Order   ☐ Credit Card

Getting Help from a Friend

 A. Complete the sentences.

1. If Ms. Arno keeps the class late, the students _____
   _____.

2. If Yolette leaves class more than five minutes late, she _____
   _____.

3. If Yolette misses her bus, she _____.

4. If Diep is late picking up her son, Hai, from day care, she _____
   _____.

5. If Ms. Arno is still talking, the students _____
   _____.

B. Think and talk about the questions.

1. How do you think the students feel when Ms. Arno keeps the class late?
2. Why is it hard for them to leave when class is over but the instructor is still talking?
3. What would you do if you had an instructor like Ms. Arno and you had to leave?

C. Think and talk about the questions.

1. Why is Diep planning to take only one course next term?
2. Why do you think she didn't know about the day care center at her school?
3. Why do you think Yolette's work-study grant ended?
4. Is financial aid available at your school? If so, what kind?
5. How do you feel about taking out a loan to pay for your education?

There are many ways to learn.
Look at the pictures and think about ways you like to learn.

Listening   Reading   Talking   Doing

Alone   In Groups   _____
(Add another way.)

Interview.

Talk to several friends. Find out if they have learned something new recently.
Ask them how they learned it.

Name	Learned	By
1. Roberto	to use a computer	doing; taking a course
2.		
3.		
4.		

A. Complete the chart.

What characteristics do hard disks and diskettes have in common?
How are they different?

Similarities	Differences

B. Find the words.

Write the words in the lecture that mean the same as . . .

1. information: _____

2. inside: _____

3. bendable: _____

4. amount that can be held: _____

5. can be carried: _____

Computers at Work

People all over the world use computers at work. Secretaries use computers to prepare letters. Accountants use computers to do bookkeeping. Even police officers use computers to keep track of crimes in their cities.

Yolette works at The Sport Shoe. She already knows how to keep the store's shoe inventory on the computer. Since computers have large memories, Yolette simply presses a button to see if she has a particular shoe in stock. She doesn't have to waste time searching for the shoes in the back room. The computer even tells her what shelf the shoes are on. Now she is learning additional computer skills so that she can help run the store more efficiently.

Diep works at City Hospital. She is learning more about computers for a similar reason. She has to analyze many lab samples every day. Her supervisor expects her to do the tests as quickly as possible. The hospital is putting in a new computer system so that laboratory workers like Diep can complete their work more efficiently.

Stan works for Manny's Landscaping Company, and he often sees his boss using various computer programs. The programs keep track of who the customers are and where they live. They also keep track of how many full-time and part-time employees are needed at different times of the year. Now Stan is learning how to use these programs too.

All of these people know one major thing: Computers can help make everyone's life much easier.

A. Check (✔) Yes or No.
Would these people use a computer at their workplace to do the following things?

	Yes	No
1. Yolette needs to know if she has a pair of red, size 8 sneakers in stock.		
2. Stan's boss wants to know how many employees he needs in August.		
3. Stan has to check a customer's address.		
4. Diep needs to order some sterilized test tubes.		
5. Yolette wants to know the names of all the shoe stores in New York City.		
6. Diep needs to analyze five blood samples.		

B. Think and talk about the questions.
1. What other ways can people use computers at work?
2. What ways can people use computers at home?

Using a Computer

One day when Yolette was working in the shoe store, Lou, the store manager, complained that too many sale fliers had been returned in the mail.

A. Write the answers.

1. What is Lou's problem? _____

2. What is Yolette's solution? _____

3. What are Yolette's reasons for suggesting the database? _____

_____

B. Think and talk about the questions.

1. What kind of employee is Yolette?
2. What kind of boss do you think Lou is?
3. How can a computerized mailing list help the business?

Stan wants to start his own landscaping company. He believes that he has the skills and energy to be a successful businessman. He wants to be his own boss within the next five years. He's even planned the name of his company—Stan Wolanski: Landscape Designs. He'll take the following steps to help him reach his goal:

1. Complete computer class this term.
2. Continue working and save $300 per month.
3. Take three courses next term.
4. Start the business sequence at the community college next year.

Stan plans to keep working and saving money while he studies. He hopes to start his business right after he graduates.

What long-term goals do you have?
Write about one of your long-term goals.

My long-term goal is to _____

_____.

To reach my goal I have to . . .

1. _____.

2. _____.

3. _____.

4. _____.

Verbs: Future Tense with *Will*/Imperatives

I He She It You We They	will 'll will not won't	write	a new program.

Will Won't	I he she it you we they	write	a new program?

Complete the conversation. Use the future tense.

Example: Yolette: _____**I'll start**_____ the new database next week.

I/start

Lou: Will it take long?

1. Yolette: I'm not sure. _____ to help.

you/have

2. Lou: _____ ?

Peter/help

3. Yolette: _____ back until Friday.

he/not be

4. Lou: _____ before then?

we/not finish

5. Yolette: I don't think so. _____ quite a while.

this/take

Take Don't take	Mr. Brown's math class next term. the statistics class this year.

Read the situation. Then tell Diep what to do. Use an imperative.

Example: Diep often wants to ask questions during class, but she doesn't know how.

_____**Raise your hand when you have a question, Diep.**_____

1. Diep wants to tell her teacher that she has a problem when class runs late.

_____

2. Diep would like to talk to other students, but she has no time right after class.

_____

Advice	You **should** take a math class.	Diep **shouldn't** miss class.
Requirement	I **have to** take math this term. Roberto **has to** take it, too.	I **don't have to** take a computer class. Diep **doesn't have to** take one, either.
	We **must** take the prerequisite.	They **mustn't** take this class yet.

Read the course description. Check (✔) the correct answer.

Basic Mathematics reviews math for business. It covers addition, subtraction, multiplication, and division of whole numbers; fractions; percents; ratios; and decimals. It uses real business problems. Prerequisite for the business sequence.

Dept.: **Math**   Cr.: **3**   Rm.: **202**
Title: **Basic Mathematics**   Instr.: **Moy**   Time: **8:30–11:30 a.m.**
Course No./Sec.: **85/01**   Day: **Mon.**

Example: Yolette wants to review percents and ratios.
_____ a. She must take Basic Mathematics.
___✔___ b. She should take Basic Mathematics.

1. Stan wants to take Small Business Practices.
_____ a. He doesn't have to take Basic Mathematics.
_____ b. He has to take Basic Mathematics.

2. Yolette wants to improve her writing skills.
_____ a. She shouldn't take Basic Mathematics.
_____ b. She doesn't have to take Basic Mathematics.

3. Roberto wants to understand practical business math.
_____ a. He should take Basic Mathematics.
_____ b. He has to take Basic Mathematics.

4. He doesn't want to study with Professor Moy.
_____ a. He mustn't take this course.
_____ b. He shouldn't take this course.

5. Roberto and Diep want to take a math class on Tuesday morning.
_____ a. They don't have to register for this course.
_____ b. They shouldn't register for this course.

1 2 3 4 5 6 7 8 9 10 11 12
What the Community Offers ■ ■ ■ ■

Getting Out in the Community

What are Stan's and Roberto's plans?

What do you think they are saying?

What is Diep's problem? What do you think she can do?

Herndon Family Recreation Center

5200 Lemon Road
Herndon, VA 22071

Herndon High School opens its doors to the community for sports and exercise programs for the entire family. The facilities are free for town residents and $3.00 a visit for out-of-town guests.

INDOOR ACTIVITIES:
- Play basketball and volleyball.
- Take exercise and dance classes, beginner through advanced. All ages welcome.
- Exercise with weights and stationary bicycle.

OUTDOOR ACTIVITIES:
- Play football, soccer, and baseball.
- Play basketball and tennis, day or night, on lighted courts.
- Run or jog on dirt track.

Open Monday through Friday 7 p.m.–10 p.m.
(except on nights of school events)
Saturdays, Sundays, and holidays 8 a.m.–10 p.m.
Call *471-9155* for additional information.

A. Check (✔) True, False, or No Information (NI).

	True	False	NI
1. The recreation center is free for everyone.			
2. Children can use the recreation center.			
3. Exercise classes are for adults only.			
4. The soccer field has lights for night games.			
5. The recreation center is closed during the school day.			
6. There is an indoor track for joggers.			

B. Think and talk about the questions.

1. Is there a recreation center or club that you can use in your community?
2. What kind of recreational activities do you like to do?
3. Where can you do them?

At the Public Library

A. Write the answers.

1. Who is Marco? _____

2. Why is Marco in Herndon? _____

3. How do Roberto and Stan know each other? _____

4. What do Stan and Marco both like? _____

5. Why did Roberto and Stan meet at the library? _____

6. Where should they go to find information about computers? _____

_____

B. Think and talk about the questions.

1. Do you ever go to your local public library?
2. Where else can you go to find information?

A. Complete the application form.

Fairfax County Public Library

To get a library card, present this application form, picture identification, and proof of address at the circulation desk.

Please print.

Name: (last) _ _ _ _ _ _ _ _ _ _ (first) _ _ _ _ _ _ _ (m.i.) _

Address: (no.) _ _ _ _ _ (street) _ _ _ _ _ _ _ _ _ _ _ _ _ _ _ _

(city) _____ (state) _ _ (zip) _ _ _ _ _

Telephone (_ _ _) _ _ _ _ - _ _ _ _   Sex: M _ F _

Soc. Sec. No. _ _ _ _ - _ _ - _ _ _ _   Birthdate: _ _ / _ _ / _ _

Signature: _____   Date: _____

B. Complete the chart.

Where can you find these materials in the library?

Herald News

History of the United States

Computers Made Easy

Webster's Dictionary

People magazine

Short Stories of the Caribbean

African Tales

Encyclopedia

_____

(Add your own.)

Newspapers/ Magazines	Reference	Fiction	Nonfiction

C. Think and talk about the questions.

1. Have you ever used the reference section? What for?
2. What other materials can you find in the reference section?

CARSON MANAGEMENT CO.
1221 Crispin Drive
Herndon, VA 22071

February 20, 2005

Ms. Diep Tran
7331 Harper Court
Apt. 2
Herndon, VA 22071

FINAL NOTICE

Dear Ms. Tran:
Your rent is two months past due. If payment is not received within five business days, eviction proceedings will be initiated.

Sincerely,

Ann Fox

Rental Manager

A. Discuss the questions.

1. What is Diep's problem?
2. How do you think she feels?
3. What can she do?
4. Where do you think she can get help?

B. Answer the questions.

1. Who did Diep call?
2. What did Diep say about her problem?
3. Why does she need an appointment before next week?
4. Why didn't she call a private lawyer?

C. Think and talk about the questions.

1. What's the difference between legal services and a private lawyer?
2. Do you know where you can get legal services in your area?

Diep earns $230 per week. She's a single parent with two small children. Is she eligible for free legal help?

LEGAL SERVICES

Legal Services will provide free legal counsel based on the following income scales, effective July 1, 2004, to June 30, 2005:

Yearly Income

Family Size	Eligibility Scale
1	$ 0 – 8,606
2	0 – 11,554
3	0 – 14,482
4	0 – 17,420
5	0 – 20,358
6	0 – 23,296

Add $2,938 for each additional person.

A. Write the answers.

1. What is Diep's family size? _____

2. If Diep works 50 weeks a year, what is her yearly income? _____

3. Is she eligible for free legal services? _____

B. Complete the sentences with *can* or *can't.*

1. Diep _____ get free legal help.

2. If you are single and earn $9,000, you _____ get free legal help.

3. A family of five _____ get free legal help if their income is $23,000.

4. A couple with no children _____ earn $11,544 and still get free legal help.

5. If there are eight people in a family and their income is $29,200, they _____ get free legal help.

C. Think and talk about the questions.

1. Have you ever used legal services or a private lawyer? Why? What were the results?

2. Do you think legal services can be as helpful as a private lawyer? Why or why not?

Taking Sides

Herndon Family Recreation Center: Growing Pains

Residents for and against the expansion of the Herndon Family Recreation Center met with the town council to present their views.

Roberto Silva, a leader of the expansion group, claims that pool renovations and a larger gym will help families spend more time together and will provide more activities for teens and young adults. "It is our civic responsibility to meet the community's needs," asserts Silva. "These changes will help the high school, too," he adds.

Anna Billman, a local store owner, opposes the expansion. She fears that too many "unsupervised young people will use the place as a hangout." The high cost of the project is another worry. "Three million dollars is too much money for recreation when fire and police protection and street repairs are being cut back," says Billman.

Backers of the expansion suggest that an additional five-percent tax on alcohol and cigarettes will raise the $3 million. Critics say that raising taxes is out of the question.

A public meeting to discuss the issue will be held next Wednesday at 7:30 p.m. in the Herndon High School gym.

Should the Herndon Town Council approve the expansion of the recreation center?

Write a list of pros and cons.

Pros	Cons

Work with a partner. One person uses Form A. The other uses Form B.
Ask your partner questions to find the missing information.

Examples: What is the phone number for Consumer Affairs?
What kinds of questions does Consumer Affairs answer?

Community Service Phone List

Consumer Affairs .... _____
answers questions about consumer
rights and responsibilities

Domestic Violence/Child Protection Services **471-9125**
examines reports of abuse or neglect of
adults and children; provides assistance
in _____

Food Stamps and WIC (Women, Infants, and Children) .... _____
decides on _____ and provides food coupons

Housing Assistance
Rent Subsidy Office **713-2134**
decides on eligibility and finds help for rent payment
Tenant-Landlord Commission .... _____
answers questions about disputes between
tenants and landlords

Job Assistance Network **481-9133**
provides job training and help in getting jobs;
offers workshops on _____
and _____

Legal Services **246-8144**
decides on eligibility and offers legal services
(except for _____ cases)

_____ **713-9150**
coordinates community programs; provides recorded
message giving dates, times, places, and fees

Community Service Agencies: Form B

Work with a partner. One person uses Form A. The other uses Form B.
Ask your partner questions to find the missing information.

Examples: What is the phone number for Consumer Affairs?
What kinds of questions does Consumer Affairs answer?

Community Service Phone List

Consumer Affairs **246-8749**
 answers questions about consumer
 _____ and _____

Domestic Violence/Child Protection Services .... _____
 examines reports of abuse or neglect of
 adults and children; provides assistance
 in crisis situations

_____

and WIC (Women, Infants, and Children)................................. **471-9147**
 decides on eligibility and provides food coupons

Housing Assistance
 _____ **Office** **713-2134**
 decides on eligibility and finds help for rent payment

Tenant-Landlord Commission **713-2155**
 answers questions about disputes between
 _____ and _____

Job Assistance Network .... _____
 provides job training and help in getting jobs;
 offers workshops on résumé writing and interviewing

Legal Services .... _____
 decides on eligibility and offers legal services
 (except for criminal cases)

Recreation Department **713-9150**
 coordinates community programs;
 provides recorded message giving

_____

Many community agencies have prerecorded telephone messages about the services they offer.

Listen and take notes.

Public Library

Hours
  Monday–Friday:
  Weekends:

Day	Time	Event
Mon., Tues.	11-12	Storytelling

Job Assistance Network

Days and Hours

Training Programs

Office Skills

Spanish
French
Russian
Japanese
Vietnamese

Practicing Your Skills

Diep and Roberto have good ideas for their community. They have both written letters to request services.

Dear Town Council Members:

I am writing to request an after-school program at the Lemon Road School. We need a program now because there are many working parents. Private after-school child care is too expensive for many parents. I think the Lemon Road School is the perfect place for an extended-day program because the school has classrooms and a playground that the children can use between 3 and 6 p.m.

I hope you will consider this request at your next town meeting.

Yours truly,

Diep Tran

To Whom It May Concern:

As a parent of two children in the schools, I believe we need more bilingual classroom aides. As you know, classes are much larger now, and the teachers do not have time for every child. Our children need extra help learning, especially English. Many immigrant parents only speak a little English, so they also need someone in the school who speaks their language.

I will present this request at the next school board meeting.

Sincerely,

Roberto Silva

A. **Do you have any ideas for your community? Prepare one of your ideas for a letter.**

Before you write, think about these questions.

- Who should I write to?
- What is my request or idea?
- What reasons can I give to support my request?

B. **Write about your idea.**

To: _____

Request/Idea: _____

Supporting Reasons:

a. _____

b. _____

c. _____

| I | **can** | | go to the Herndon Center today. |
| He | **can't** | | |

| Where | **can** | they | go to play tennis? |

A. Use the flyer on page 19. Complete the sentences. Use *can* and an appropriate verb.

Example: Roberto's brother from Atlanta _____*can go*_____ to the center.

1. Roberto and his brother _____ all day there on Saturday.

2. But they _____ tennis if it rains.

3. They _____ baseball either.

4. They _____ on Monday morning to exercise.

5. But they _____ weights on Monday night.

B. Use the chart you completed on page 21. Write questions with *Where*.

Question	Answer
Example: ____*Where can Roberto use a dictionary?*____ Roberto/dictionary/use	In the Reference Room.
1. _____ you/sports scores/read	In the newspaper area.
2. _____ Marco and Stan/computer books/find	In the Nonfiction stacks.
3. _____ Diep/fairy tale books/borrow	In the Fiction section.
4. _____ someone/videos/look for	On the second floor.

Reported Speech with *That*

A. Check (✔) the sentences that show reported speech.

_____ 1. I went to a meeting about the recreation center last night.

_____ 2. This expansion is very necessary for a strong Herndon.

_____ 3. Roberto said that better facilities will help families spend time together.

_____ 4. He added that the improvements will help the high school, too.

_____ 5. Anna Billman doesn't like the idea of a bigger recreation center.

_____ 6. She says that it will create problems for storekeepers.

_____ 7. She also claims that the cost is too high.

_____ 8. But I don't agree with her.

B. Read this conversation between Diep and Roberto. Then rewrite sentences using reported speech.

Example: Roberto: Where were you this morning?
　　　　　　Diep: I had an appointment with Legal Services.

　　　　　　Diep **_says that she had an appointment with Legal Services._**

1. Roberto: Who did you see there?
　　Diep:　　I met with Mr. Russell, a lawyer.

　　Diep _____

2. Roberto: What did he do for you?
　　Diep:　　Mr. Russell called the bank and my landlord.

　　Diep _____

3. Roberto: How did that help?
　　Diep:　　The bank checked their records. I won't be evicted!

　　Diep _____

4. Roberto: I'm happy it worked out.

　　Roberto _____

5. Diep:　　I'm very happy too.

　　Diep _____

1 2 3 4 5 6 7 8 9 10 11 12
Making Ends Meet ■ ■ ■ ■ ■ ■ ■

Bills, Bills, and More Bills

How do you think Yolette and Al feel?
Why do you think they have so many bills?
What can they do?

Monthly Expenses

A. Fill in the monthly budget worksheet for the Jamisons.

Monthly take-home pay:		
Yolette	$ 935.10	
Al	$1,142.27	
Total	$ 2,077.37	

Expense:	Amount Due	
1. rent	$ 712	
2. electricity	_____	
3. phone	_____	
4. heat	_____	
5. _____	_____	
6. _____	_____	
Subtotal:	_____	

Credit card:	Total Amount Due	Minimum Payment Due
7. County Bank Card	_____	_____
8. _____	_____	$15
9. _____	_____	$15
Subtotal:	_____	_____
TOTAL:	_____	_____

B. Write the answers.

1. What's the total amount Yolette and Al owe? $_____
2. What's the minimum they must pay now? $_____
3. How much will they have left over for living expenses? $_____

C. Think and talk about the questions.

1. Do you think Al and Yolette have other regular expenses?
2. How can Yolette and Al avoid owing so much money in the future?
3. Can you think of ways to save money and pay all your bills?

Al and Yolette usually spend all of their income each month, so they seldom have any money left. Their monthly living expenses are quite high, and they often spend their money on unnecessary things. They want to be able to save some of their money so that Yolette can visit her elderly parents in Haiti and so that they can make a down payment on a new home. They have to learn how to manage their money more efficiently.

Recently Al read an interesting article about money management in a magazine. He thought that it contained a lot of useful information that could help them save some money.

Saving Money—A Common Sense Approach

"There is no such thing as a typical budget," reports Gail Browning, author of *Managing Your Money Wisely*. "A young couple without children usually has low housing costs, but spends a lot on clothing and entertainment. A family with several children generally pays much more for housing and has less money to spend on other things."

People need to evaluate how they spend their money. According to Ms. Browning's book, one of the tricks of managing money wisely is to spend money in the most practical way. Consumers should think about every purchase they make. They should also consider their long-range goals on a regular basis, because day-to-day purchases can really add up and take away from savings.

Ms. Browning suggests that consumers use the following quiz to see if they should or should not make a purchase.

Ask yourself:	Yes	No
1. Do you really need this item?		
2. Is the price reasonable?		
3. Have you looked in other stores and compared prices?		
4. Is it the best time to buy this item?		
5. If this is a bargain, is it a current model?		
6. Do you need all the features of this item?		
7. If the price is high, will this item really satisfy you?		
8. Can you trust the retailer (store)?		

Score your answers:
If you answered *yes* 6–8 times, buy the item.
If you answered *yes* 4–6 times, think about the purchase again.
If you answered *yes* 0–4 times, don't buy the item.

Think about a purchase that you would like to make soon. Then take the quiz.

When to Pay Bills

It's March 29. Diep Tran deposited a paycheck recently, and she won't get another one until next week. She has a lot of bills, but she doesn't have enough money to pay all of them right now.

Help Diep decide which bills to pay now and which bills to pay later.

A. Look at Diep's bills.

Write *1* next to the bills Diep should pay now.
Write *2* next to the bills that she can pay after her next paycheck is deposited.

___ **Greater Washington Electric:**
$32   Due: 4/15

___ **Carson Management Co.**
Rent due April 1: $528

___ **Acme Insurance Co. Term Insurance**
Premium due April 10: $36

___ **Barron's Discount Stores**
OVERDUE NOTICE
If your minimum payment of $25 is not received by April 3, the entire amount of $68 will be due immediately.

___ **COUNTY BANK** *CAR LOAN*
Payment 16 due April 1: $45

B. Complete the register for all the bills you marked with a *1*.

Check Number	Date	Description of Transaction	Amount of Withdrawal (−)	Amount of Deposit (+)	New Balance 397.52
	3/24	paycheck deposit		230	
121					
122					
123					
124					

Reading a Utility Bill

A. Figure out how much Roberto owes.

Sherwood Energy Company

Account Number: 3864A/Silva, R.   Date of Invoice: 3/28/05   Invoice: 32974

Product	Price	Quantity	Amount	Previous Balance	Total Due
#4 Fuel	.849/gal.	140 gal.	$_____	$58.00	$_____

_____ **Check here if you want to participate in our monthly budget plan.**

Dear Mr. Silva,

   Thank you for your inquiry into the Sherwood Energy Company's Budget Plan. With budget billing, Sherwood Energy estimates your annual fuel bill based on the previous year's bills. Then we break the bill into 11 equal payments for July through May. In June, you receive a bill for the remainder of your balance or a refund.

   We have calculated your regular bill over the past year and provided a Budget Plan estimate.

R. Silva's bills for 2003–2004   Total: $644

July: $23	Aug: $23	Sept: $24	Oct: $25	Nov: $47	Dec: $70
Jan: $106	Feb: $107	Mar: $91	Apr: $65	May: $38	June: $25

R. Silva's budget billing based on last year's total of $644.

July: $58	Aug: $58	Sept: $58	Oct: $58	Nov: $58	Dec: $58
Jan: $58	Feb: $58	Mar: $58	Apr: $58	May: $58	June: $_____*

* This amount will vary based on your use and price fluctuations.

B. Write the answers.

1. What amount will Roberto probably owe in June? _____
2. What's Roberto's average monthly cost for heat over 12 months? _____

C. Think and talk about the questions.

1. Are utility bills a big part of your monthly budget?
2. How can you save energy and money?

COUNTY BANK *CREDIT CARD*

ALBERT AND YOLETTE JAMISON

ACCOUNT NUMBER: X401 6553 73123	CREDIT LIMIT	NEW BALANCE	AVAILABLE CREDIT	PAYMENT DUE DATE	MINIMUM AMOUNT DUE
	$1500	1492.95	7.05	4/30/05	$45.00

DATE	DESCRIPTION	CHARGES	CREDITS
02 28	LL JONES RESTAURANT	22.95	
03 02	PAYMENT—THANK YOU		−100.00
03 08	GARNET EATERY	31.95	
03 09	SELWYN'S TV SHOP	198.99	
03 15	SOUTHWEST AIRLINES	456.00	
03 16	GLORIA'S SHOES		−22.00
03 16	RAY'S GIFTS	12.75	
03 17	DELTA RESTAURANT	17.95	
03 18	DELTA RESTAURANT	19.95	
03 19	DELTA RESTAURANT	20.95	
03 20	DELTA RESTAURANT	15.95	
03 23	COUNTY BANK CREDIT CARD MEMBERSHIP FEE	20.00	
03 25	WAYLAND BED & BREAKFAST MOTEL	362.52	
03 25	*FINANCE CHARGE*	6.01	

ACCOUNT SUMMARY						
PREVIOUS BALANCE	PAYMENTS	CREDITS	NEW PURCHASES	FINANCE CHARGE	OTHER CHARGES	NEW BALANCE
				APR: 16.8%		
428.98	(100.00)	(22.00)	1159.96	6.01	20.00	$1492.95

A. Write the answers.

1. What was the Jamisons' biggest vacation expense? _____

2. How much did the Jamisons pay to eat out in March? _____

3. How much did they pay of their previous balance? _____

4. How much is the membership fee? _____

B. Think and talk about the questions.

1. Why do you think Al and Yolette received a credit from Gloria's Shoes?

2. What are some advantages of having a credit card?

3. What are some disadvantages of having a credit card?

Understanding Credit Terms

Understanding Credit Terms

37

COUNTY BANK *Credit Card*
CREDIT CARD TERMS AND INFORMATION SUMMARY

Annual Membership Fee: This fee will be charged to your account. It will appear on your statement on your anniversary date, one year from the date your account was opened or renewed.

Monthly Payments You Must Agree to Pay:

Balance	Minimum Monthly Payment
$0–$14.99	amount of balance
$15–$500*	$15
over $500*	3% of your balance, rounded up to the nearest dollar

*You may pay all or part of your balance at any time, as long as you pay your minimum monthly payment.

Finance Charge: You will be assessed an ANNUAL PERCENTAGE RATE (APR) of 16.8% (1.4% per month) on all unpaid balances. You can avoid additional finance charges by paying off your New Balance before the Payment Due Date.

Problems or questions about your bill? Send inquiries to:

CBCC
Box 8221
Hanover, PA 17333-8221, or call 1-800-712-0009.

Be sure to include the following information:
1. Your name and account number
2. The item in error and an explanation of the problem

* *

A. Complete the sentences.

1. If the Jamisons owed $130, the minimum payment would be _____.

2. To avoid a finance charge now, they will have to pay the entire bill by _____.

3. Because the Jamisons' bill is over $500, what percentage of the balance do they have to pay? _____

B. Think and talk about the questions.

1. Why do you think banks make you pay finance charges?
2. What are the risks of using a credit card too often or for expensive purchases?

The Phone Bill

Here's part of the Jamisons' phone bill. They're trying to figure out when to call their families and friends for the least amount of money.

MATC **Mid-Atlantic Telephone Company**
page 2 of 2

Itemized Account of Service

No.	Date	Time	Place		Area-Number	*	Min.	Amount
1.	MAR 9	716 PM	MIAMI	FL	305-472-0090	ED	3	1.66
2.	MAR 13	730 PM	PAPRINCE	HT	509-785-9098	STD	15	18.23
3.	MAR 19	730 PM	BKLYN	NY	718-879-1440	ND	10	5.73
4.	MAR 26	1006 PM	PAPRINCE	HT	509-785-9098	ECN	15	11.00
5.	APR 3	740 PM	BRONX	NY	718-678-4472	ED	3	2.02

Calling Card 703-893-4741

No.	Date	Time	Place		Area-Number	*	Min.	Amount
6.	MAR 19	630 PM	BRONX	NY	718-678-4472	EC	2	1.59
			FROM SOUTH IS	FL	813-543-5111			

Total Amount 40.23

* Discounted rates within US:
  ED Evening Dial   EC Evening Calling Card   ND Night/Weekend Dial
Calling rates outside US: STD Standard   ECN Economy

A. Check (✔) True, False, or No Information (NI).

	True	False	NI
1. This bill is three pages long.			
2. The Standard rate to Haiti is cheaper.			
3. Yolette could have saved more than $7 on her first call to Haiti.			
4. Within the United States, daytime rates are the most expensive.			
5. The discounted calling times inside and outside the United States are the same.			
6. Calling during discounted times saves money.			

B. Think and talk about the questions.

1. Do you make long-distance calls?
2. Who do you call? How often do you call?
3. Do you try to call during discounted times? Why or why not?

Al found a mistake on his telephone bill.
He called the telephone company to correct the error.

A. Listen to two different versions of Al's telephone conversation. Think and talk about the questions.

1. What did Al say that was different in the second conversation?
2. How did Al make you feel in each conversation?
3. How do you think the operator felt in each conversation?
4. Which conversation would you like to have?

B. Write the answers.

1. How would you describe Al in the first conversation? _____

_____

2. How would you describe Al in the second conversation? _____

_____

3. What evidence did Al and Yolette have that they weren't home to make the

call? _____

_____

Why People Save

People save for different reasons. Diep wants to take more courses at school. She also has to buy clothes for her two children frequently because they grow so fast. Even though she only buys secondhand or discount clothes, she often has to buy on credit. She worries that occasionally she will need money for an emergency. She puts $30 each week in a savings account. Having a savings account that grows regularly makes Diep feel much better.

Yolette and Al think about the future too. They'd like to have a little nest egg so that they can own their own home someday. Yolette also wants to visit her parents in Haiti. Al and Yolette know that sometimes they spend money on things they don't need or don't use. They've decided to use their credit cards for emergencies only. After they pay off their credit card bills, they are going to put money away from each paycheck. They've set a goal for themselves to pay off their credit card bills in five months. Then they intend to save $1,000 within a year.

Find the words.

Write the word or phrase in the story that means . . .

1. used or worn by someone else first: _____

2. very often: _____

3. once in a while: _____

4. an unexpected problem or crisis: _____

5. at equal times: _____

6. money saved for the future: _____

A. Read Al's letter to his sister and brother-in-law.

April 17, 2005

Dear Jack and Marta,

It was good to see you when we were in Florida. You must be surprised to get a letter from me instead of a phone call. It's part of our new campaign to be more careful about money. We're trying to save some money so that we can put a down payment on a house and so Yolette can visit her parents in Haiti this summer.

We are trying to change a lot of our habits so that we can save. For instance, we're not eating out as often as we used to. Instead, we eat at home, and we've found out that we both enjoy cooking. I think we're eating better than we ever did! We're also trying to find inexpensive activities — like hiking and going to the community recreation center for sports—so that we don't spend as much on entertainment. The next time you see us, we'll probably be in great shape.

I hope you can visit us soon. Give the kids a big hug from Uncle Al.

Al

B. What are your plans or ideas about ways to save money? Write a letter to a friend or relative.

Include the following information.
- Describe how you plan to save money.
- Tell why you want or need to save.
- Identify what you expect to happen if you follow your plans.

Adverbs of Frequency

0% ← ——————————————————————→ 100%

never at no time not once	rarely seldom hardly ever	sometimes occasionally now and then	often frequently many times	usually generally regularly	always every time constantly

Complete the sentences with an appropriate adverb from the chart.

Example: Diep's children are __constantly__ (99%) growing.

1. They _____ (55%) outgrow their clothes.

2. They _____ (10%) wear clothes for a whole year.

3. They _____ (85%) need clothes every few months.

4. She _____ (45%) shops at Your Turn, a secondhand store near the hospital.

5. Your Turn _____ (75%) has good school clothes.

6. But it _____ (0%) carries winter coats.

7. For winter coats, Diep _____ (100%) goes to Barron's Discount.

8. She shops at the end of the season and _____ (80%) gets a double discount.

9. The children _____ (65%) need new shoes twice a year.

10. Diep _____ (5%) buys expensive shoes for them.

11. They _____ (100%) outgrow shoes so fast!

Advice	What bills **should** Diep **pay** today?	**Should** she **pay** these bills today?
Ability	What bills **can** I **pay** next week?	**Can** I **pay** those bills next week?

Roberto and Adela are looking at new cars. Write questions with *can* or *should*.

Example: Adela: ____What model should we get____ ?

                                    model/get

1. Adela: _____ with better mileage?

                        look at/one

   Roberto: That's a good idea. Let's talk to a salesperson.

2. Adela: We like this model. But _____?

                                        choose/a different color

   Salesperson: Oh yes, it comes in six different colors.

3. Roberto: How much _____ for our old car?

                              trade-in/offer

   Salesperson: Let me check that out for you.

Underline the irregular verbs. Then write the base form of each verb.

Example: Al and Yolette <u>said</u> they are changing their spending habits.   ____say____

1. They began to pay off their credit card bills.   _____

2. They took a cooking course at the adult education center.   _____

3. They found out about free entertainment in their area.   _____

4. Al didn't make a lot of long-distance calls.   _____

5. Instead, he wrote letters to his friends and relatives.   _____

6. They thought their budgeting worked well.   _____

7. They soon paid off their credit cards and started to save.   _____

1 2 3 4 5 6 7 8 9 10 11 12
Living with Machines ■ ■ ■ ■ ■ ■ ■

What's the Problem?

How do Roberto and Yolette feel?

What can they do?

Have you ever had a problem with a machine?

Trouble with Machines

A. Answer the questions.

1. Roberto took one friend's advice. It didn't work well. What was the advice?
2. Another friend gave him good advice. What was it?
3. What problem did Yolette have with the printer?
4. What does she say about machines? Do you agree?

B. Interview.

Talk to several friends. Find out if they've ever had a problem with a machine. What did they do?

Name	Problem	Solution
1.		
2.		
3.		
4.		

C. Think and talk about the questions.

1. What kinds of machines do you use?
2. How do you feel when a machine doesn't work?
3. What do you do when a machine doesn't work?

Connecting the New VCR

Roberto bought a VCR. His son, Eddy, read the manual while Roberto tried to connect the equipment. Roberto had repaired many TVs and radios in his shop in Puerto Rico, so he felt that he understood that kind of mechanical equipment. He thought that he didn't need the manual. The VCR was more complicated than Roberto expected. Two hours later he was feeling angry and frustrated because the VCR still didn't work. He wanted to return it to the store.

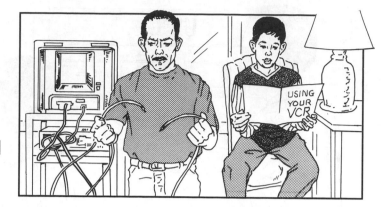

Eddy finished reading the manual. He untangled the cables and wires, following the directions and diagrams in the manual. Soon the VCR was connected, and Eddy was recording a movie for his little sister, Cruz.

Roberto was frustrated that he couldn't connect the VCR, but he was very pleased that Eddy had helped him. Now the entire family can watch or record shows anytime they want.

A. Read these words that can describe Eddy and Roberto. Check (✔) if a word describes Eddy, his father, or both.

Add two more words that describe one or both of them.

	Eddy	Roberto	Both
1. careful			
2. stubborn			
3. satisfied			
4. annoyed			
5. patient			
6.			
7.			

B. Think and talk about the questions.

Do you like people to give you advice when you are working on a difficult problem? Why or why not?

Roberto wants to watch the basketball game on channel 2. Adela, his wife, wants to see a cable TV movie that's playing at the same time on channel 36. They've decided to watch the game and record the movie for later. Roberto and Eddy are figuring out how to watch one show and record another one at the same time.

A. Listen to Eddy's directions and take notes.

1. _Turn on the VCR and insert a new tape._
2. _____
3. _____
4. _____
5. _____
6. _____
7. _____

B. Use your notes to correct the mistakes.

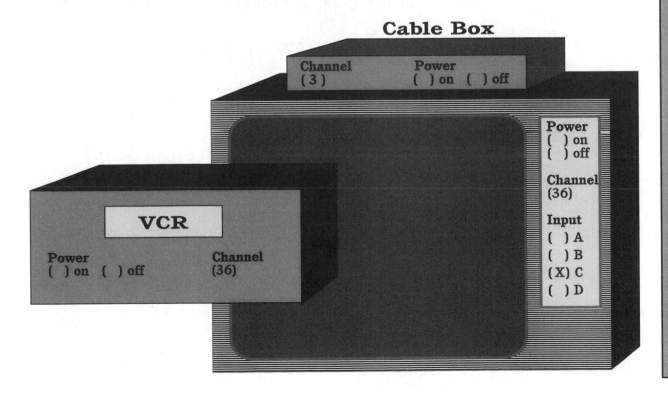

Cable Box

Channel
(3)

Power
( ) on ( ) off

Power
( ) on
( ) off

Channel
(36)

Input
( ) A
( ) B
(X) C
( ) D

VCR

Power
( ) on ( ) off

Channel
(36)

Limited One-Year Warranty

Holmes Electronics Corporation

Keep this portion of the warranty for your records.

1. Fill out and return the Warranty Registration Card (the perforated bottom half of this card) **within 10 days of your purchase.**

2. This warranty applies only to repair or replacement of the VCR if it is defective in material or workmanship. Damage from unreasonable or abusive use or commercial use is not covered by this warranty.

3. All parts of this VCR are guaranteed for a period of one year, as follows:

   a. Holmes will repair or replace this VCR if you return it to our factory, freight prepaid, with a proof of purchase (a dated receipt) and $22.50 for handling and return shipping charges.

   b. When returning the VCR, pack the item carefully, in its original carton if possible. Be sure to attach a tag to the item with your name, address, and phone number. We recommend that you insure the package. Mark the outside of your package **"Attention Repair Dept."** and ship to:

   Holmes Electronics Corp., 78 Broad Street, Dunhill, NC 28334.

Complete this story. Use the information on the warranty card.

Roberto completed the _____ card and _____ it within

1   2

three days. Six months later, the VCR stopped recording TV programs. Sometimes

it would switch channels on its own. Roberto had kept the warranty _____

3

with his important papers. He read it again and decided to _____ the

4

VCR to the manufacturer for repairs.

He didn't have the _____ carton, but he found a sturdy one that

5

was the right size. He packed it _____ and _____

6   7

a tag labeled according to the directions. He also sent a check for _____

8

and the proof of _____, which was his _____ from

9   10

the store.

Work with a partner.
One person uses Form A.
The other uses Form B.

Yolette and Roberto are both
having computer problems.
They're helping each other
in the computer lab.

You are Yolette. Your partner is Roberto.

Yolette can't get the printer to work correctly. Roberto is checking
the User's Guide and giving Yolette some suggestions.

A. Tell your partner about your computer problems and ask for advice.

1. The printer won't work. Ask what button to press.
2. Ask how to reset the printer.
3. You want to print in a vertical page format and the printer
   is printing horizontally.
4. Now the print is too light. Ask what to adjust.
5. The print is still too light. Ask what to do next.

Now Roberto is trying to clean the mouse for his computer.
Yolette is reading about the procedure in the User's Guide.

B. Find the information for your partner in the steps below.
   (Note: The steps are not in the correct order.)

a. Gently shake the mouse until the ball drops out of its socket.
b. Point to an object on the screen by moving the mouse.
c. Use a cotton swab dipped in alcohol to loosen the lint on the rollers.
d. Turn off the computer when you clean the mouse.
e. Use adhesive tape to pick up the dust and lint on the ball.
   Wipe out the dirt inside the socket.
f. Turn the mouse over so that the ball is face up and remove the cover.

Work with a partner.
One person uses Form A.
The other uses Form B.

Yolette and Roberto are both
having computer problems.
They're helping each other
in the computer lab.

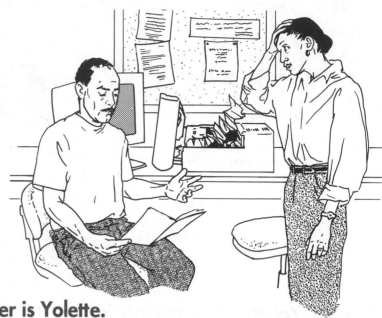

You are Roberto. Your partner is Yolette.
Yolette can't get the printer to work correctly. Roberto is checking
the User's Guide and giving Yolette some suggestions.

A. Find the information for your partner in the steps below.
(Note: The steps are not in the correct order.)

a. To change the page format, press the page-orientation switch.
b. Adjust the darkness control.
c. Hold the Start/Stop button, and then press and release the Print/Check
   button to reset the printer.
d. Replace the toner cartridge.
e. Press the Print/Check button if the printer doesn't work. The printer may
   have to be reset.
f. Change paper trays.

Now Roberto is trying to clean the mouse for his computer.
Yolette is reading about the procedure in the User's Guide.

B. Tell your partner about your computer problems and ask for advice.

1. Ask if the computer needs to be on or off when you clean the mouse.
2. Ask how to hold the mouse when taking off the cover.
3. Ask how to get the ball out.
4. Ask how to clean the mouse.
5. Ask what to do about the lint that is on the rollers.

Stan is on his way to work. He wants to pick up some lunch and eat it on the way. But first Stan must stop at the cash machine at his bank. He wants to withdraw $10, but he needs to check his balance first. His special password is PILA. That's the name of his hometown in Poland.

WELCOME TO
GREATER WASHINGTON
SAVINGS BANK.
INSERT YOUR CARD,
MAGNETIC SIDE DOWN.
ENTER YOUR
FOUR-DIGIT PASSWORD.

1	2 ABC	3 DEF
4 GHI	5 JKL	6 MNO
7 PRS	8 TUV	9 WXY
*	0	#

SELECT YOUR
TRANSACTION:
■ DEPOSIT
■ TRANSFER
■ WITHDRAWAL
■ BALANCE
■ CANCEL

YOUR BALANCE IS
$45.90

PLEASE WAIT WHILE
YOUR TRANSACTION
IS BEING PROCESSED.
REMOVE THE MONEY
FROM THE BIN BELOW.
REMOVE YOUR CARD
FROM THE SLOT.

A. Write the answers.

1. What numbers did Stan enter?

_____

2. What did Stan select first?

_____

3. What is Stan's next transaction?

_____

B. Find the words.

Write a word in the story or on the screens that means the same as . . .

1. put in:

_____

2. choose:

_____

3. type in:

_____

4. deposit, transfer, or withdrawal:

_____

5. prepared:

_____

6. take out:

_____

Accidents Happen

A. Stan isn't in class today.
   Put this story in order to find out what happened to him.

____ While Stan was pulling it free, he cut himself on the sharp blade.

____ He showed his bloody arm to the foreman, who almost passed out.

____ Stan had to drive himself to the emergency room.

____ Stan was trimming some thick hedges with an electric hedge trimmer.

____ Stan went back to work to fill out an accident report, but the foreman had gone home earlier.

____ He was also given a tetanus shot.

____ The trimmer got caught in some tangled branches.

____ It took 10 stitches to close the cut.

_9_ After the foreman left, the crew gave themselves the afternoon off.

B. Create a new ending to the story.

Start with the sentence that reads, "He was also given a tetanus shot," and make up a new ending to this story.

C. Think and talk about the questions.

1. Why did Stan have to fill out an accident report?
2. Have you ever had an accident? What happened?

Stan and his supervisor, Bert Daley, had to fill out an accident report after Stan cut himself while trimming a hedge. This is part of their report.

Manny's Landscaping Company
Injury Report

EMPLOYEE: Complete this section.

Job Title: _landscape assistant_   Date of Injury: _5/19/05_   Time: _10:30 a.m._

Place of Accident: _52 Crosby Road, Reston, VA_

Source of injury: _Machine. Cut by hedge trimmer blade._

Treatment by: ☐ screening clinic ☑ emergency room ☐ rehabilitation
☐ other _____

SUPERVISOR: Complete if the employee accident involved one or more of the following:

☑ injuries involving one day or more of lost time   ☑ medication required
☐ burns of second or third degree   ☐ embedded foreign bodies
☑ lacerations requiring stitches   ☐ back strains

Nature of injury (burn, fracture, etc.) and body parts involved: _cut on left arm_

Name(s) of witness(es) to injury: _Pete Ditter, Frank Ward_

▶ Listen to the two descriptions of the accident.

1. Choose the important facts that Stan mentions.
   Write a statement that he might write.

   EMPLOYEE'S STATEMENT: _____

   _____

   _____

   _____

2. Choose the important facts that Bert mentions.
   Write a statement that he might write.

   SUPERVISOR'S STATEMENT: _____

   _____

   _____

   _____

Practicing Your Skills

Roberto and Adela taught their children, Eddy and Cruz, to help around the house. Eddy likes to cook. Last night he decided to make fish for dinner. Adela left him some directions for using the microwave. Here's what she wrote:

1. Unwrap the frozen fillets and put them on a glass plate.

2. Select DEFROST on the microwave, then push two minutes.

3. When the timer beeps, turn the plate halfway around and defrost for three more minutes.

4. Let the fish stand in the microwave for five minutes. Then wash the fillets in cold water and pat them dry with a paper towel.

5. Arrange the fish in a layer in the glass baking dish on the counter. Squeeze lemon juice on the fillets, and cover the dish loosely with plastic wrap.

6. Select HIGH on the microwave, push three minutes, then push START.

7. When the timer beeps, open the door and CAREFULLY remove the plastic wrap. (It can be hot.) If the fish doesn't flake apart easily, cook on HIGH for another 15 to 30 seconds. Wait three to five minutes before removing the fish from the microwave.

Write directions.

Choose a household appliance or machine that you use (washing machine, coffeemaker, computer, cash register, etc.) and write directions so that a friend can operate it.

_____

_____

_____

_____

_____

_____

_____

Active	Passive
Stan <u>deposited</u> money in the ATM. The janitor <u>picked up</u> the papers.	Money <u>was deposited</u> in the ATM. The papers <u>were picked up</u>.

Write the sentences in the active voice.

Stan went to the bank.

Example: A paycheck was deposited.   *He deposited his paycheck.*

1. His bankcard was inserted into the slot. _____

2. Instructions were seen on the screen. _____

3. The Deposit button got pushed. _____

4. The amount was keyed in. _____

5. The paycheck was inserted into a slot. _____

6. The receipt was taken from the machine. _____

Circle the words that describe the picture below and the people in it. Then complete the sentences.

angry	cheerful	cozy	frustrated	helpful
jammed	messy	pleased	satisfied	smiling

1. This workspace is _____.

2. The paper is _____ in the printer.

3. Yolette is _____ by the problem.

4. Roberto is trying to be _____.

5. Machines that don't work can make anyone _____.

Reflexive Pronouns/Verbs: Past Tense

Singular	myself	yourself	himself, herself, itself
Plural	ourselves	yourselves	themselves

Complete the sentences with a reflexive pronoun.

1. I tried to connect our new VCR by _____.

2. You'll have trouble if you try to do it by _____.

3. We often think we can do everything _____.

4. Eddy read the manual _____.

5. Cruz is learning to operate the VCR by _____.

6. Soon my wife and kids will be using the VCR all by _____.

Rewrite the directions in the past tense.

Example: Push the Open button and insert a CD.

Eddy _____ **pushed the Open button and inserted a CD.** _____

1. Close the lid and push On.

   He _____

2. Push Search to find the song you want to hear.

   He _____

3. Hit the Play button to listen.

   Then he _____

4. Don't leave your compact disks in the player.

   Eddy _____

5. Store CDs in their boxes.

   He always _____

1 2 3 4 5 6 7 8 9 10 11 12

Travels in America ■ ■ ■ ■ ■ ■ ■ ■

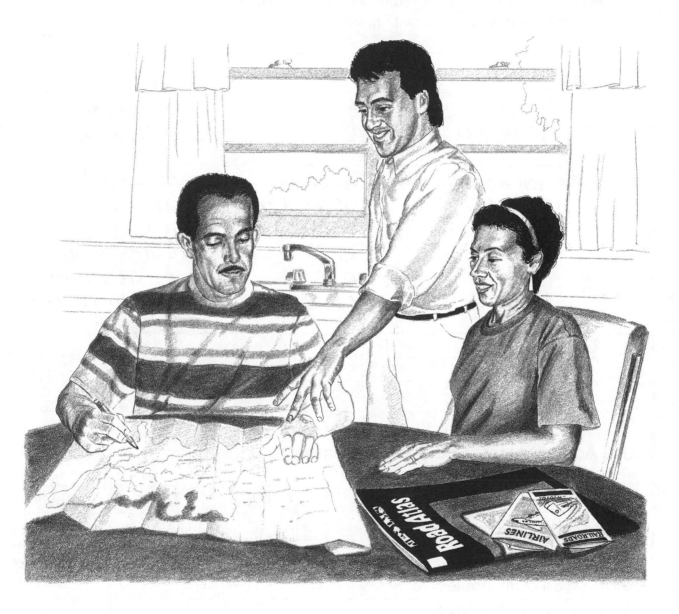

Planning a Trip

What do you think the Silvas are going to do?
Have you ever planned a trip? Where did you go?
How did you plan your trip?

Comparing Transportation

Roberto and Adela are going to visit relatives in Atlanta. They are taking Eddy and Cruz with them. Marco is going on the trip too. He's excited about seeing his family again. The Silvas want to know the best way to go to Atlanta.

Adela called the airport, train and bus stations and made some notes. She wants to share the information with the family.

Plane	Train	Bus
9:00, 11:30 2:45, 5:00, 7:30	Lv. daily @ 11:00	8:00, 10:00, 2:00, 6:00
Nonstop 2 hrs. $238 round-trip kids full fare	Coach $108 one-way $135 round-trip kids 2-15 ½ price Extra $ for sleeping car 14 hrs.	Change in Richmond 2 hr. layover 16 hr. trip Can go through different cities Can interrupt trip anywhere $87 one-way $150 round-trip kids ½ price

Use Adela's notes. Check (✔) the answer.

Which way is . . .

	Plane	Train	Bus
1. the fastest?			
2. the slowest?			
3. the most comfortable?			
4. the least comfortable?			
5. the most expensive?			
6. the cheapest (round trip)?			
7. the most flexible (time)?			
8. the most flexible (route)?			

A. Answer the questions.

1. What advice does Stan give Roberto?

2. What does Diep suggest to Roberto?

3. What do Stan and Diep say about Great Smoky Mountains National Park?

4. What does Roberto think about their suggestion?

5. What are some of the reasons Stan and Diep give for going by car?

6. What states do the three friends mention in their conversation?

B. Write the answers.

1. What services does Stan's auto club provide? _____

   _____

   _____

2. How much is a single membership? _____

   a single membership with a student discount? _____

   a family membership? _____

Mapping a Route

Roberto convinced Adela and Marco that a car trip would be best. Use the story below to trace the route they plan to take from Washington, D.C., to Atlanta, Georgia.

Complete the story.

Roberto told his family,

"First we'll travel _____ to
                        east, west, north

Strasburg, Virginia. Then we'll go

_____ through
southeast, northeast, southwest

Lexington and _____,
                Greensboro, Roanoke

Virginia, and Bristol, Tennessee.

We'll continue driving _____, until we get to Kodak,
                        southeast, southwest, northwest

Tennessee. Turning _____ will takes us right into Gatlinburg,
                    west, north, south

Tennessee, and Great Smoky Mountains National Park on the border of Tennessee

and North Carolina. After a few days in the Great Smokies, we'll go

_____ to Commerce, Georgia. In Commerce, we'll pick up the major
north, south, east

highway that goes _____ right into Atlanta."
                  southwest, southeast, northwest

Many Miles to Go

Roberto examined a chart on his map that listed the mileage from one city to another. It gave him a general idea of how many miles his trip would be. Then he showed the chart to Cruz, who began planning their next trip right away. She wanted to visit her cousins in Miami and her aunt and uncle in New York City. After that, she wanted to go to Disneyland, with a side trip to a great science museum in Chicago she'd heard about.

Roberto loved her plans, but he said they would involve too much driving. He showed her just how many miles her trips would take.

Driving Distances for Cruz's Vacation Plans						
	Atlanta	**Chicago**	**Los Angeles**	**Miami**	**New York City**	**Wash., D.C.**
Atlanta	XXX	583	1,935	610	747	542
Chicago	583	XXX	1,741	1,190	711	594
Los Angeles	1,935	1,741	XXX	2,355	2,446	2,295
Miami	610	1,190	2,355	XXX	1,095	927
New York City	747	711	2,446	1,095	XXX	204
Wash., D.C.	542	594	2,295	927	204	XXX

A. Use the chart to calculate the trips Cruz wants to take.
1. Washington, D.C.–Miami–New York City–Washington, D.C., is _____ miles.
2. Washington, D.C.–Los Angeles–Chicago–Washington, D.C., is _____ miles.

B. Use the chart to complete the sentences.
1. The cities that are farthest apart are _____ and _____.
2. The cities that are closest together are _____ and _____.

C. Check the answers.
1. Which trip is the shortest distance?

___ Miami to Atlanta to Los Angeles

___ Washington, D.C., to New York City to Chicago

___ New York City to Chicago to Washington, D.C.

2. Which trip is the greatest distance?

___ Atlanta to Washington, D.C., to Los Angeles

___ Chicago to Miami to New York City

___ Los Angeles to New York City to Atlanta

What's the Weather Like?

The Silvas are leaving for their trip in the morning. They plan to drive through Virginia and part of Tennessee. They expect to arrive at Great Smoky Mountains National Park on Friday. They will spend their weekend touring the park before they leave to visit their relatives in Atlanta.

Adela and Roberto listened to the news to find out about the weather in the places they are going on their trip. They also looked at a weather map in the newspaper.

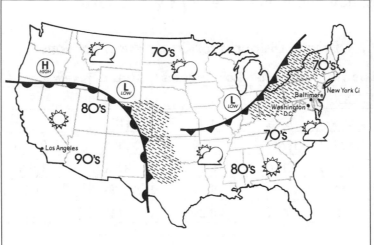

A. Check (✔) True or False.

	True	False
1. The high in Washington was 79°.		
2. The cold front is bringing sunshine to the Washington area.		
3. It will probably rain in Washington on Thursday morning.		
4. The sun will probably shine in Washington on Friday.		
5. Virginia is cloudy and overcast.		
6. The rain will end by Thursday afternoon.		
7. It's been a very hot summer in Tennessee.		

B. Think and talk about the questions.

1. Do you listen to the weather forecasts on the radio or TV?
2. Where could you find out about weather and temperatures outside of your area?
3. What's the weather forecast for today where you are?
4. Are the weather forecasts always right?

Packing for the Trip

63

All of the Silvas are busily packing their suitcases for their trip.
Even Cruz is trying to pack her own suitcase. She made a list
of what she needs to bring with her.

pajamas	underwear
jeans	swimsuit
T-shirts	cookies
red dress	doll
snowsuit	toothpaste
boots	umbrella
mittens	sneakers

A. Help Cruz pack for the trip.

1. Underline the things that you think Cruz should take.
   Put an X through the things that she doesn't need.
2. Make a list of other things that you think Cruz should take.

_____   _____

_____   _____

B. Make a list of other things that the Silvas should take on their trip.

Clothing	Toiletries	Other Necessities
socks	comb	flashlight

A Night Out

The Silvas arrived in Gatlinburg, Tennessee. They checked into a nice motel and decided to stay there a couple of days while they visited Great Smoky Mountains National Park. Marco offered to take care of Cruz and Eddy so that Adela and Roberto could go out alone. They wanted to have a special time together, but they didn't want to spend too much money. They looked through the brochure of activities in the area.

Dixie Gardens. This theme park and craft center provides thrilling rides, live craft demonstrations, picnic facilities, and a petting zoo to ensure fun for all ages. Open daily 9–9, June–Aug. Restricted schedule other seasons.
ADMISSION: adults, $19.75; children 4–11, $14.25
PARKING: $2

Great Smoky Roundup. Nightly performances include music, comedy, and Wild West fun! A sing-along fest is followed by rodeo demonstrations and contests. Regional and country specialities make dinner a treat. Shows begin nightly at 7 p.m. Dinner served continuously from 6 p.m. Open mid-Mar. through Dec.
ADMISSION: adults, $24.50
children 4–11, $15.25

Mountainview Music Theatre. See local and professional talent perform bluegrass, country, gospel, and pop music. Monday through Saturday at 8:15 p.m. from mid-May through October. Matinees Wednesdays and Saturdays at 2:30 p.m.
ADMISSION: adults, $9; adults over 55, $7, children 7–12, $5.
(Not recommended for children under 7.)

Think and talk about the questions.

1. Where do you think Roberto and Adela went while Marco took care of Eddy and Cruz? Why do you think they picked that activity?
2. What attractions would appeal to you? Why?
3. Do you think these activities are worth the money they cost?
4. How can you find out about less expensive activities when you take trips?

Protecting the environment will be the theme of the coming year at Eddy's school. He wants to learn about the national park so that he can report about his trip when he goes back to school. He has learned a lot from reading a pamphlet called *An Introduction to the Great Smokies*.

WELCOME TO GREAT SMOKY MOUNTAINS NATIONAL PARK

The Great Smoky Mountains National Park covers over a half-million acres in North Carolina and Tennessee. It was named for the blue, smoky haze that almost always covers its peaks. Many summits rise over 6,000 feet and are home to some of the most varied plant life in the hemisphere. There are 180,000 acres of virgin forest, with thousands of evergreen and deciduous trees. Other plant life includes wild rhododendron, myrtle, azalea, dogwood, and wild flowers in profusion.

Hunting was banned in the Great Smokies in 1934. Wildlife is abundant and includes deer, grouse, wild turkey, and bear. Miles of hiking trails and paved roads provide access to the wonders of nature in the park.

The Great Smoky Mountains National Park is open all year, and admission is free. Lodging is available atop Mount LeConte and at many campgrounds in the park. Hikes on many trails and lectures by park rangers are available during the main tourist seasons. Horses can be rented for trail rides at several stables. Mount LeConte offers magnificent views. Newfound Gap Road is a scenic road that crosses the park. Miles of streams provide excellent trout fishing.

A. Write your answer.

What things would you like to do in the Great Smokies?

_____

_____

_____

B. Discuss the question.

How can national parks help protect the environment?

Asking for Directions

The Silvas want to go to the Foster Historical Museum, but they aren't sure how to get there.

A. Listen to the conversation and trace the route.

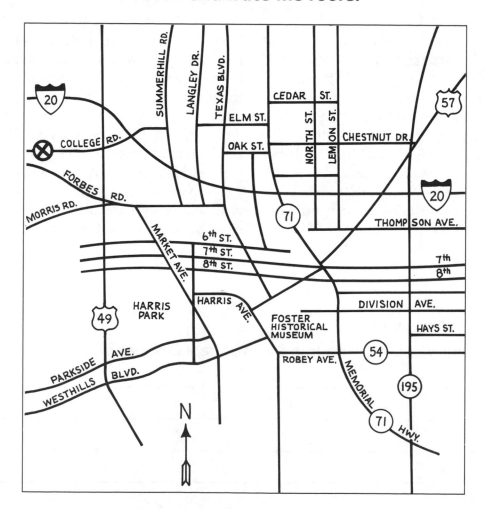

B. Plot another route to the museum.

Give directions to a friend to see if your directions are clear to someone else.

Dear Stan,
  You were right about Smoky Mts. National Park! We all loved it! We took a trail ride by horseback up Mt. LeConte. The scenery was spectacular! We took several hikes with a park guide who taught us a lot about the geography and history of the region. Eddy was so interested that he started collecting rocks from the region. The weather was good, and we went swimming every day. Cruz is ready to move down here permanently. Hope you're not working too hard!
                              Roberto

Stan Wolanski
42 Baxter Road
Herndon, VA 22070

Write a postcard to a friend or relative.

Tell about a trip or vacation that you've taken or that you'd like to take.

How much/many? = specific number or general amount (6 shirts, several miles, all) How far? = distance (two feet, a short distance, 100 miles, to Tennessee)	
How many postcards do you want?	I want a dozen.
How much do they cost?	They're 25¢ each.
How far is the post office?	It's two blocks from here.

Match the questions and answers.

1. How many people will go on the trip?
2. How much is an adult ticket?
3. How much time does it take?
4. How far will you have to walk?
5. How many cities will you visit?
6. How far is the motel from the train station?

a. It's about ten blocks away.
b. Four of us.
c. About a mile.
d. Eight hours.
e. $65.
f. We'll go to three.

Use the prepositions and phrases to complete the sentences.

across	behind/in back of	close to/near	in front of	inside	next to

1. The woman is _____ the car.

2. The Silvas are _____ their car.

3. Roberto and Adela are sitting _____ Cruz.

4. They are sitting _____ each other.

5. Cruz is _____ her parents.

6. The woman is pointing _____ College Avenue.

Adjectives: Superlatives

tall	taller	the tallest
cheerful	more cheerful	the most cheerful
slim	slimmer	slimmest
friendly	friendlier	friendliest

A. Complete the sentences with the superlative form.

Example: The Southwest has _____ **the highest** _____ (high) temperatures in the country.

1. It also has _____ (dry) weather.

2. The North Central states have _____ (heavy) snowfalls.

3. They often have _____ (wet) springs, too.

4. The South usually has _____ (mild) winters.

5. But it often has _____ (humid) summers.

6. The Northwest usually has _____ (rainy) weather in the nation.

7. But it also has _____ (green) summers.

B. Write sentences with superlatives.

Example: ___ **Adela is the neatest and the slowest packer** ___ in the family.

Adela/neat/slow/packer

1. _____ when she travels.

She/new/clothes

2. _____ in the family.

Cruz/fast/packer

3. _____ , too.

She/messy/careless/one

4. That's because _____ of the family.

she/impatient/member

Verbs: Past Tense in Time Clauses

> **While Roberto tried to connect the VCR**, Eddy read the manual.
> Eddy read the manual **while Roberto tried to connect the VCR.**
>
> **Before I worked full-time**, I had a part-time job.
> I had a part-time job **before I worked full-time**.
>
> **After his boss passed out,** Stan drove himself to the hospital.
> Stan drove himself to the hospital **after his boss passed out.**
>
> **When Diep got home,** she called her brother.
> Diep called her brother **when she got home.**

A. Underline the time clause in each sentence.

1. After Diep finished work, she stopped at the bank.

2. She deposited her paycheck after she paid her bills.

3. Before she left, Diep checked the balance of her savings account.

4. When she left, she took a brochure about long-term savings.

5. She read the information while she waited for the bus.

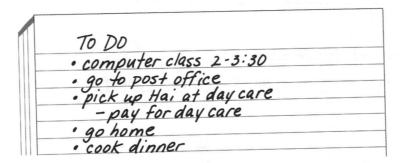

```
TO DO
• computer class 2-3:30
• go to post office
• pick up Hai at day care
   -pay for day care
• go home
• cook dinner
```

B. Read Diep's TO DO list from last Friday.
   Complete the sentences. Use time clauses in the past tense.

1. Diep went to the post office after _____.

2. Before _____, she got stamps and mailed some letters.

3. She gave a check to the day-care worker when _____.

4. After _____, she went home.

5. Her son watched TV while _____.

How far?	= distance (10 miles, 2 blocks, 100 yards)
How long?	= length of time (2 hours, 15 minutes, 7 days, a month); measurement (3 feet, 5 meters)
How often?	= frequency or number of times (every 15 minutes, once a day, twice a week)

How far is it from New York to Miami? It's about **1,500 miles**.
How long is the trip by car? It takes about **28 hours**.
How often do you call your relatives in Florida? I call **every Saturday**.

Eddy gave a report to the class about his family's trip.
The other students asked some questions.

A. Match the questions with the answers.

1. How far is it from here to the Great Smoky Mountains?
2. How long did it take you to drive there?
3. How often did you get to stop and see things?
4. How long has the park been open?
5. How often does it rain there?

a. every two or three hours
b. several times a week
c. two days
d. about 400 miles
e. almost 70 years

Another student in Eddy's class went to Atlanta by bus.

B. Write a "How" question for each of the answers about the trip.

1. _____?
   We were on the bus for about 15 hours.

2. _____?
   Atlanta is about 500 miles from here.

3. _____?
   The bus stopped only two times.

4. _____?
   We stayed in Atlanta for a week, and then we took a trip to the ocean.

5. _____?
   It takes about four hours to drive to the coast.

Two-Word Verbs: Separable

check out	= look at, explore	**put away**	= save, put in its place
fill out	= complete, write all the responses	**send out**	= mail
keep away	= not go near something	**turn off**	= stop some kind of power
look up	= use a book to find information	**turn on**	= start some kind of power
pay off	= pay the complete amount owed	**work out**	= arrange a plan
pick up	= get someone or something	**write down**	= write notes on paper

Eddy **looked up** <u>information</u> on the Great Smoky Mountains for a school report.
Eddy **looked** <u>information</u> **up** on the Great Smoky Mountains for a school report.
Eddy **looked** <u>it</u> **up** for a school report.

Bert Daley bought a new lawn tractor for the company.
He told Stan to learn how to use it.

A. Match the written instructions for the lawn tractor with another way of saying them.

1. Look at the machine to detect any loose parts.
2. Push "Power" to start the machine.
3. Make sure the tractor doesn't run over any sharp objects.
4. Complete the warranty card.
5. Stop the machine if there is a problem.

   a. Keep it away.
   b. Turn it off.
   c. Check it out.
   d. Turn it on.
   e. Fill it out.

Bert is talking to Stan about the new equipment.

B. Use the separable verbs to complete the sentences.

1. *Bert:* "Stan, how did you know how to set up this machine?"

   Stan: "I _____ (look up) in the manual."

2. *Bert:* "What do you do to start it?"

   Stan: "You _____ (turn on) with this switch."

3. *Bert:* "I don't see the warranty card here. Where is it?"

   Stan: "I think your secretary's going to _____(send out) today."

4. *Bert:* "We should save these instructions. I'll _____ (put away) in the office."

break down	= stop operating, stop working	**go over**	= study or review
cut back	= reduce or lower (the amount)	**keep on**	= continue
eat out	= buy meals at a restaurant	**move in**	= begin living in a place
get along	= manage, meet one's needs	**run into**	= meet by chance
get off	= leave (the bus or train)	**run out of**	= use up the supply
get up	= rise from bed	**watch out**	= be careful

Examples: Diep gets up at about 5:00 in the morning.
Will Stan keep on working for Bert?
I have to get off the bus at Center Street.

Yolette and Al talked about ways to reduce their expenses.

A. Rewrite the sentences, using inseparable verbs.

1. Tomorrow morning we'll rise from bed early and start making a plan.

   _____

2. We need to lower the number of long-distance phone calls.

   _____

3. We need to stop eating at restaurants so much.

   _____

4. We need to continue saving money.

   _____

5. We need to review our budget from time to time.

   _____

6. Let's hope the car doesn't stop working. That would ruin our budget.

   _____

B. Complete the sentences, using inseparable verbs.

1. Yolette and Al know they have to _____ on their spending.
2. They'll _____ for unnecessary expenses.
3. They don't want to _____ money.
4. They'll just have to _____ on a tight budget.

Bert paid the money to the men **who (that)** did the work. =
Bert paid the money to the men. The men did the work.

Here is a book **which (that)** describes the Great Smoky Mountains. =
Here is a book. The book describes the Great Smoky Mountains.

Yolette and her boss Lou are talking about the new customer database.

A. Fill in the first word of each dependent clause: *who, that,* or *which.*

1. *Yolette:* "Lou, are there any other names _____ should be added to the mailing list?"

2. *Lou:* "The customers _____ came in yesterday should probably be included."

3. *Lou:* "I left the information _____ you need next to the computer."

   Yolette: "Thanks. I want to finish the list this morning."

4. *Lou:* "Do you think we can try to get the addresses of customers _____ buy children's shoes?"

5. *Yolette:* "Sure. I'll do it right after I input the names _____ you just gave me."

B. Combine the two sentences, using dependent clauses.

Example: Yolette: "The salesman was very nice. He gave me directions."
Yolette: "*The salesman who gave me directions was very nice.* "

1. Yolette: "Here's the list of people. The people buy children's shoes."
   Yolette: "_____"

2. Lou: "The list looks good. You made the list."
   Lou: "_____"

3. Lou: "OK, here are the fliers. They need to be sent out."
   Lou: "_____"

4. Yolette: "I know the man. He designed and printed the fliers."
   Yolette: "_____"

5. Yolette: "Mr. Jones is a friend. You can trust him."
   Yolette: "_____"

1 2 3 4 5 6 7 8 9 10 11 12

Problems on the Job ▪ ▪ ▪ ▪ ▪ ▪

Making Mistakes

What's happening here?
How do you think Roberto feels?
What should he do?

Roberto's Apology

A. Write the answers.

1. Why did Roberto apologize to the customer? _____
_____

2. How did the customer respond? _____
_____

3. What did Roberto tell the customer to do? _____
_____

4. What did Roberto offer the customer? _____
_____

B. Answer the questions.

1. How do people apologize? What do they say?
   How do people accept apologies?

   Write different ways to . . .

apologize	accept an apology

2. What happens when people don't want to accept an apology?
   What kinds of things can they say or do?

C. Complete the sentence.

How do you feel when something goes wrong?
Complete the sentence below. You can give more than one answer.

When something goes wrong, I feel _____
_____
_____
_____.

Marcel Dulac manages the restaurant. Marcel is worried that Mr. Jansen won't eat there again because of what Roberto did.

A. Listen to two versions of the conversation between Marcel and Roberto. Think and talk about the questions.

1. What did Roberto say that was different in the second conversation?
2. How did Marcel treat Roberto in each conversation?
3. How do you know which conversation was more successful?

B. Describe Roberto in . . .

conversation 1	conversation 2
1.	
2.	
3.	

No Promotion for Diep

Diep has worked at City Hospital for two years. She has worked hard at her job and has always tried to improve her skills. She enrolled in computer classes so that she would be even more efficient at work. Diep hoped that she would receive a promotion, or at least a raise, and she was very upset when she didn't get either one. She tried to understand why.

When Diep talked to her brother Quang about it, he got angry. He said she was being discriminated against. He thought she was passed over because she was a woman. But Diep said that her supervisor was also a woman. Quang got angrier. He said she didn't get the raise because she was Vietnamese. Diep said other Vietnamese workers got promotions and raises, so that couldn't be the reason either.

"Ms. Morris is just not satisfied with my work," Diep said sadly. "If I spoke English better, she'd give me a promotion. If I understood directions better, I'd do things faster. If I worked more hours, she'd take me more seriously."

Quang said, "You always work hard. You never miss work. You're never late or rude. You have to tell your supervisor that you deserve a promotion and that you need that raise."

Diep thought Quang was right, but she didn't think she could tell her supervisor. She thought she would have to look for another job.

A. Answer the question.

What would you do if you didn't get a raise or promotion that you thought you deserved?

_____

_____

B. Interview.

Talk to a friend or someone in your family.
Ask him or her to complete these sentences.

1. If I were late for work, _____.

2. If I disliked my boss, _____.

3. If _____, I'd quit my job.

4. I'd look for another job if _____.

A. Check (✔) True, False, or No Information (NI).

	True	False	NI
1. Diep can give out patient information.			
2. Diep read the patient's file.			
3. Doctors and nurses are authorized to give out patient information.			
4. Diep was polite to the man.			
5. The man was polite to Diep.			

B. Match the sentences that have the same meaning.

1. I beg your pardon?   **a.** Why do you think that?

2. I'm authorized.   **b.** Excuse me? Say that again, please.

3. That's our work policy.   **c.** It's private and personal.

4. What gave you that idea?   **d.** I'm permitted or allowed.

5. That's confidential.   **e.** It's company procedure.

Performance Evaluation

Here is Diep's job evaluation. What kind of worker is she?

CITY HOSPITAL

Employee's Name **Diep Tran** Current Position **Lab Ass't.**

Dept. **Laboratory** Supervisor **Joan Morris**

Please rate all criteria **1–5** (lowest to highest) or **N/A** in each category.
For promotions, required criteria marked (**R**) cannot be rated **N/A**.

• knowledge of work (R)	1	2	3	4	(5)	N/A
• quantity of work (R)	1	2	3	(4)	5	N/A
• accuracy of output (R)	1	2	3	4	(5)	N/A
• 15 hours of computer training (R)	1	2	3	4	5	(N/A)
• good patient contact	1	2	(3)	4	5	N/A
• problem solving	1	2	3	(4)	5	N/A
• adheres to hospital policies (R)	1	2	3	4	(5)	N/A
• uses independent judgment	1	2	(3)	4	5	N/A
• completes paperwork accurately and in a timely fashion	1	2	3	4	(5)	N/A
• plans own work efficiently	1	2	3	(4)	5	N/A

Overall evaluation (check one)

____ Consistently exceeds expectations

✓ Fully meets expectations

____ Meets some expectations

____ Does not meet expectations

Supervisor recommends (check one)

✓ Step promotion to **2/0** job category

____ Continue in present job category

____ Additional supervision/training

____ Termination

Recommendation: ☐ approved ☑ rejected

A. Write the answers.

1. Why didn't Diep get the promotion? _____

2. What should she have told Ms. Morris? _____

B. Think and talk about the question.

What would you do about a problem like this?

Timely Tips for Meeting with Your Supervisor

Is it time for your annual job review? Whether you're a counter clerk or a crew chief, there are standard questions that you can expect every time. Here's what to expect and how to make the most of your time with your supervisor.

• What do you already know how to do well?

This is your opportunity to shine! Point out what you do well, what you enjoy doing, what you've trained others to do, and so on. If you don't feel comfortable bragging, think about *what you'd like to hear* someone say about your work and tell *that* to your supervisor.

• What would you like to do better in this job?

Admit that there's always room for improvement. Show that you're aware of your (minor) weaknesses and let your supervisor know how you've already started to work on them. Don't be ashamed of mistakes or problems. Just show that you're aware of them and are doing something about them.

• What new tasks would you like to do or to learn next?

You need to figure out your *own* goals to answer this one. Are you happy where you are, doing what you're doing? Do you want a change, new challenges, or a promotion? These questions should be answered in your mind *before* the performance review. This is a chance for you to remind your supervisor of what you've already accomplished and stress that you want to advance. If possible, show how your goals will benefit the company (or better yet, the supervisor).

It also helps to have some questions for the supervisor. Ask how you can improve your performance and what your chances are for getting new responsibilities. Finally, be sure to thank your supervisor at the end of the interview. You always want to end a meeting on a positive note.

A. Think and talk about the questions.

1. Do you agree with the advice in this article?
2. Think about your job or one that you've had.
   How would you answer the questions if you had a job review?

B. Choose one of the questions from the article.
   Write an answer that you'd give to your supervisor.

_____

_____

_____

Hot under the Collar

What do you think happened?

A. Check (✔) the answer.

Who . . .

	Stan	Frank	Pete
1. trimmed the hedges too low?			
2. told Stan he'll help cover up the mistake?			
3. won't help cover up the mistake?			
4. thinks Bert won't check the work order?			
5. makes fun of Stan?			

B. Think and talk about the questions.

1. Why is Stan so mad?
2. What would you do in a similar situation? Why?
3. What might happen if the owner of the house or Bert Daley did notice the mistake?
4. Did anyone ever ask you or someone you know to cover for another person? What was the situation?

Stan wants to be a crew supervisor. He works hard, but lately other crew members have been complaining about his temper. He feels that he gets angry only because they provoke him. They also say he's not cooperative. He feels that his co-workers don't take their jobs as seriously as he does and that they don't work very hard. Bert Daley just wants to get the work done. He doesn't want to get in the middle of Stan's conflicts with other workers. Here is Stan's latest job evaluation.

MANNY'S LANDSCAPING COMPANY
Job Evaluation

E = Excellent   S = Satisfactory
U = Unsatisfactory

Employee: *Stan Wolanski*   Date: *9/15/05*   Years with Company: *1*
Position: *gardener*   Name of Evaluator: *Bert Daley*

Rating		Additional Comments
E	general work habits	*hard worker, never have to tell him anything twice*
S	maintains tools, equipment	
S	keeps tools, truck, shop neat	
S/U	uses good judgment	
U	uses equipment appropriately and carefully	*careless use of hedge trimmer cost him five days work in May*
E	adheres to schedule	
E	gets to work on time	
S/U	accepts additional hours	*often unavailable during school times*
E	maintains good relationships with customers	*outstanding skills w/ customers*
S/U	supervisor	
U	co-workers	

Evaluate Stan.

Do you think Stan would make a good crew supervisor? Write his strengths and weaknesses below. Then decide if he would make a good supervisor and talk about why you made your decision.

Strengths	Weaknesses

How Do You Act under Pressure?

Roberto, Diep, and Stan all act differently during difficult situations. The list below gives some of the words that describe how people act when they are under pressure or embarrassed.

A. Write the words that you think describe each character. Then write the words that describe the way you act.

Add some words of your own.

becomes shy	gets angry	is thoughtful	gets embarrassed
avoids situations	argues back	defends self	apologizes
accepts apologies	thinks out solutions	stays calm	gets confused
annoys others	makes situation worse	improves situation	_____
_____	_____	_____	_____

Roberto	Diep	Stan	Me

B. Interview some friends or members of your family. Write their answers.

Name	What would you do if a co-worker asked you to do something dishonest?
1.	
2.	
3.	
4.	

A. Read this letter in the advice column "Dear Gabby."

Dear Gabby,

I am the manager of a very elegant restaurant. I only allow smoking in the smallest, least pleasant area of the restaurant. When customers who smoke come in and are seated there, they usually complain and want to sit in the nonsmoking area. Or when the smoking area is full, they don't want to wait and insist on sitting in the nonsmoking area. These customers often demand ashtrays or drop ashes on their plates. Then my nonsmoking customers complain that they can't breathe. I believe that "the customer is always right." My problem is, which customer? How can I handle my customers and keep them all happy?

Confused Manager
Des Moines, IA

B. What would you do?

Answer the letter to "Dear Gabby." Use the questions to help write your letter.

- What could the manager do when someone wants to smoke in a nonsmoking area?
- Would you allow ashtrays in nonsmoking areas?
- Which customers do you agree with?
- Would you change the areas of the restaurant so smokers would feel more comfortable?
- Explain any ideas you have for solving this problem.

Dear Manager,

_____

_____

_____

_____

_____

_____

Sincerely,

_____

(your name)

Verbs: "Unreal" Conditional

I'd feel happy **if** I **had** a good job. (would feel)	I **wouldn't be** happy **if** I **lost** my job. (would not be)
If Marco **had** a good job, he**'d feel** happy. (would feel)	**If** he **lost** his job, he **wouldn't be** happy. (would not be)

A. Complete the sentences with a verb from the box.

not be	explain	✔get	look	tell	take

Example: Diep would feel better if she _____**got**_____ a promotion.

1. She _____ for another job if she felt unappreciated.

2. If Diep asked, Mr. Myers _____ his recommendation.

3. If Mr. Myers explained the evaluation, Diep _____ so upset.

4. If Diep _____ Mr. Myers about the computer course, she'd receive a promotion.

5. Mr. Myers wouldn't be happy if Diep _____ another job.

B. Imagine you work in a restaurant. Answer the questions. Use an unreal conditional.

What would you do . . .

1. if a customer complained about your service?

   _____

2. if a customer said you'd brought the wrong sandwich?

   _____

3. if a customer asked for extra salad?

   _____

4. if a customer didn't leave a tip?

   _____

He **should have been** careful with the saw.

They **should have talked** to their supervisor.

You **shouldn't have left** early yesterday.

Think about the story on page 82. Listen to the tape again if necessary. Complete the following sentences.

Example: Pete __shouldn't have asked__ (not ask) Stan to cover for Frank's mistake.

1. Frank _____ (read) the work order.

2. He _____ (do) the work more carefully.

3. He and Pete _____ (not trim) the hedges so low.

4. Stan _____ (not yell) at them.

5. He _____ (not make) Frank angry.

6. The three co-workers _____ (find) a better solution.

Check the polite form.

Example: _____ a. Excuse me, but it's your fault.
    __✔__ b. Perhaps we can find a solution together.

1. _____ a. Pardon me. Please let me help with that.
   _____ b. Here! Give it to me!

2. _____ a. That's very kind of you.
   _____ b. Yeah, thanks.

3. _____ a. I want you to help me now.
   _____ b. Excuse me, may I ask you a question?

4. _____ a. You can't have that! That's none of your business.
   _____ b. I'm not authorized to give out that information.

5. _____ a. I appreciate your position, but I really need to see those forms.
   _____ b. They're mine, and I demand that you give them to me right now.

1 2 3 4 5 6 7 8 9 10 11 12
Saving the Environment ■ ■ ■ ■ ■ ■

At the Recycling Center

What are Cruz and Eddy doing?

What is Adela doing?

Does your town recycle?

What can you recycle? What can't you recycle?

Why Do We Sort Trash?

**A. Listen to the conversation and read the signs.
Then complete the sentences.**

1. Adela complained that there are too many _____.

2. Eddy and Cruz explained that _____.

3. Adela agreed that washing bottles _____.

4. Eddy said that separating items keeps _____.

5. He explained that tape can _____.

6. Eddy told her that the problem is called _____.

7. When Adela was young, _____.

B. Answer the questions.

1. What products with the recycling symbol have you seen?

_____ _____ _____

2. What products that have the recycling symbol do you use?

_____ _____ _____

A Guide to Recycling

Herndon and its residents are working together to save the environment. This guide is a reminder of what items you can place in your recycling bins. Put the bins next to your trash can on your regular trash pickup day.

WHAT CAN BE RECYCLED?

	Yes			No
Clean clear, brown, or green glasses and jars	✔		Window glass, light bulbs, mirrors	✘
Metal food and beverage cans, and clean aluminum foil	✔		Toxic waste containers	✘
Clean, crushed plastic bottles and jugs only, no caps	✔		Plastic bags, Styrofoam	✘
Newspapers, glossy magazines, and catalogs	✔		Phone books, junk mail, waxed cardboard, and envelopes	✘

printed on 100% recycled paper

Check the items that can be recycled.

	Yes	No
1. an olive jar		
2. a cardboard cereal box		
3. aluminum foil		
4. a soda can		
5. an empty can of paint		
6. the Herndon *Daily Times*		
7. a car windshield		

A. Write the answers.

1. What kind of packaging does Roberto think is unnecessary? _____
   _____

2. Who pays for the extra packaging?
   _____

3. What did Adela do in Puerto Rico that's also environmentally sound here?
   _____
   _____

B. Write the answers.

Here are some ideas for saving energy and cutting down on waste. What are they?

  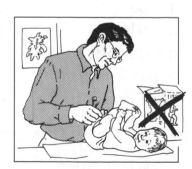

_____   _____   _____

C. Prepare a list.

What environmentally sound practices from your native country do you think should be used in the United States?

_____   _____

_____   _____

_____   _____

_____   _____

A Field Trip

Each child in Cruz Silva's class had to do a project about helping the environment. Cruz and several of her classmates decided to form a team and participate in Herndon's Annual Riverbank Clean-up Project.

The Clean-up Project had three purposes: to pick up trash on the riverbank, to reduce pollution in the river, and to recycle as much of the trash as possible. Cruz and her friends each used a large bag to pick up various items on the riverbank. They had separate bags for glass; for plastic; for items that can be reused or returned, such as deposit bottles and cans or usable sports equipment; and for items that cannot be recycled or reused.

Here's some of what they found. Put each item in the right bag.

1 shoe	a bicycle tire	a shoelace
a pickle jar	18 deposit cans	2 tennis balls
a juice bottle	a torn sweatshirt	a plastic football
5 gum wrappers	11 deposit bottles	an empty detergent bottle
2 plastic milk bottles	a broken fishing pole	an empty jug of windshield cleaner

Glass That Can Be Recycled	Plastic That Can Be Recycled	Items That Can Be Reused or Returned	Items That Cannot Be Recycled or Returned

Cruz and her classmates had to write a report about helping the environment. The teacher gave them several environmental problems. She asked the students to interview their family and friends to help find some solutions to the problems.

Interview. Then complete the class reports.

Each problem is followed by one solution. Interview some friends or family members and record their solutions.

Water Conservation: How to Use Less and Keep It Pure

Name	Solution
Roberto	*Motor oil and paint can poison the drinking water, so don't pour them down the drain.*

Air Pollution: How Can We Make the Air Better to Breathe?

Name	Solution
Adela	*Organize a car pool or use public transportation instead of driving alone.*

Energy Conservation: The Less We Use, the More We Save

Name	Solution
Eddy	*Replace regular bulbs with energy-efficient bulbs. They cost more to buy, but they last longer and save money on your energy bills.*

MediKit Deserves to Build

MediKit Deserves to Build

There has been a lot of discussion about the pros and cons of allowing MediKit Technical International to build a new facility in Herndon. MediKit is pressing the Herndon Town Council to grant the permits it needs to begin building. Meanwhile, the town council is currently considering whether or not to grant MediKit the permits.

The development of a new biotech industry in Herndon is wholly beneficial to our community. MediKit produces a valuable medical product: sterile blood-test kits for medical laboratories in the mid-Atlantic states. MediKit's choice of Herndon as the site for expanding production can only offer our community more jobs, a wider tax base, and greater economic stability.

Some in the community fear that a company which uses chemicals in a manufacturing process is a potential air or water polluter. They don't know MediKit. MediKit's president, Alfred Gomez, assures us that almost 50 years in the business has given the company the opportunity to learn how to reuse or recycle all possible components of its chemical products.

MediKit has chosen three undeveloped acres in southeast Herndon as its new site. This is another example of the corporation's sensitivity to the community. MediKit has assured the town council that it will not contribute to the traffic problems in our densely populated town.

A spokesperson for MediKit estimates that the company will provide up to 500 direct jobs for local citizens and almost as many indirect jobs to support those employees, in such fields as food service, construction, personal service, and education. The effect on the economy will be profound. MediKit estimates that between one and two million dollars a year will be pumped into the local economy. These are numbers that we should not ignore. We urge the town council to grant the necessary permit for our new neighbor to commence operations speedily.

Opponents of this permit are sensible people. Once MediKit specifies how it recycles and disposes of its waste and people understand the multiple benefits of a new, local company, we believe these reasonable people will surely change their minds.

Think and talk about the questions.

1. How does this editorial try to persuade the Herndon Town Council to grant the permit for MediKit?
2. Where did most of the facts from this editorial come from?
3. How does the editorial deal with its opponents?
4. Can you think of any reasons to disagree with the editorial?

A. Listen to the conversation between Stan, Diep, and Roberto.

Take notes on the pros and cons that they mention.
The first one is done for you.

Name	Pros	Cons
Diep	makes good medical products	

B. Think and talk about the question.

Do you think the Herndon Town Council should grant the permit to MediKit?
Why or why not?

Hazardous Waste: Handle with Rubber Gloves

A. Answer the questions.

1. What hazardous substances does Stan want to dispose of?
2. What steps should Stan take when he's disposing of hazardous household substances?

B. Think and talk about the questions.

1. What hazardous household substances do you have at home?
2. How do you dispose of them?
3. Can you think of any ways to reuse or recycle them?

C. Complete the story.

Richard Rivera works for MediKit. He said that the _____ of chemicals

1

his company uses has _____ 85 percent since 1949. Most of the

2

_____ that MediKit now uses are nontoxic and nonpolluting. The

3

_____ chemicals that MediKit does use are _____ of by high

4 5

temperature incineration. Talk-show host Ron Fisher asked if incineration

_____ the ozone layer or causes acid _____. Rivera said that

6 7

there were _____ with incineration but it was better than _____

8 9

disposal. He also mentioned the motto _____, Reuse, and Recycle.

10

There are some problems that must be solved before the Herndon Town Council will permit MediKit to build its new plant.

A. Read each problem and think about possible solutions. Then write your ideas for each one.

1. The narrow, two-way streets around MediKit's proposed site cannot handle the increased traffic of employees commuting to work and trucks carrying materials in and out of the factory.

   Possible solution(s): _____

   _____

   _____

2. Daytime truck noise and factory noise will interfere with activities in the senior center across from the new site.

   Possible solution(s): _____

   _____

   _____

3. MediKit would have to cut down an extra acre of trees in order to build the planned on-site day-care center for employees' children.

   Possible solution(s): _____

   _____

   _____

B. What else can MediKit do to help the community? Write your idea.
   Explain what it will require and how it will benefit the town and/or the company.

   _____

   _____

   _____

   _____

Practicing Your Skills

Dear Hospital Employees:

City Hospital announces a $100 reward to Diep Tran for her winning idea for reducing waste in our hospital. Congratulations, Ms. Tran!

Here is Ms. Tran's winning application. Her idea will be implemented immediately.

Name: Diep Tran

Employee #: 021323

Idea for Conservation:

Every month, some department changes a form, promotes someone and prints new letterhead, or computerizes information and discards stacks of file cards. I suggest we donate the old forms, letterhead, and file cards to local public schools. They can use old forms to practice math problems, use the backs of letterhead to photocopy messages home to parents, and use file cards to make flash cards. Not only do we reduce paper and help supplement school budgets, but every time the paper is reused, someone is reminded that City Hospital cares about our schools and environment.

Imagine that your town offers a prize for the best way to start or improve recycling in your area.

Write your idea here.

Here are some questions that will help.

- What's the idea?
- What aspect of the environment does it help?
  (saving energy or other resources, reducing pollution, reducing trash)
- How would it work?
- Who would be involved?
- How much would it save (or cost)?
- Are there any other benefits from this idea?

_____

_____

_____

_____

I You We They	**have**	**recycled**	newspapers every week.
He She It	**has**	**done**	it for many years.

**Complete the paragraph with verbs in the present perfect.
Then write about yourself.**

Cruz and Eddy's school _____**has held**_____ an Environment Day program
                                hold

for several years. The school _____ all students to participate.
                                    encourage

The students _____ their parents to help, too. Each grade
                    ask

_____ one issue. Eddy's grade _____ on
        choose   work

reducing electricity usage in their school and homes.

Eddy _____ a usage-savings chart with three friends.
            make

They _____ directions for their chart. Each student
            write

_____ a chart home. All the groups _____
        take   develop

good ideas. One group _____ the lights with lower-watt bulbs.
                            replace

Another _____ reminders to shut off lights in empty rooms.
                draw

How have you helped the environment?

_____

Modals: *Should, Must/Have to/*Reported Speech

I You He She It We They	**should**	<u>reuse</u> paper bags.

I You We They	**have to/must**	
He She It	**has to/must**	<u>recycle</u> newspapers.

Rules for Herndon's Trash and Recycling Station

▶ Herndon residency required for Trash and Recycling permits.
▶ Brush and tree stumps can be no longer than 4'.
▶ Please rinse all bottles, cans, and plastics before recycling.
▶ Dispose of lightbulbs and ceramics with trash. Do not recycle.
▶ Please put deposit bottles and cans in specially marked bins.
▶ Tie or bag magazines and newspapers before recycling.
▶ Disposal of hazardous waste or batteries is prohibited at this Station.

Complete the sentences. Use *should* or *must/have to, has to.*

1. Al and Yolette _____ live in Herndon to use this Station.

2. Al _____ cut up a 6' branch before he throws it away.

3. He _____ keep deposit bottles separate from other glass.

4. Yolette _____ wash out her cans before recycling them.

5. Al _____ put a broken mixing bowl in his trash.

What did Cruz tell her mother? Use reported speech.

Example: recycling rules

      <u>Cruz told her mother that recycling rules are important.</u>

1. dirty bottles or cans

_____

2. leaving caps on bottles

_____

1 2 3 4 5 6 7 8 9 10 11 12
Real Costs of a Car ■ ■ ■ ■ ■ ■ ■ ■ ■

Checking Out a Car

Where are Adela and Marco?
What do you think happened to the car?
How do you think they feel?

On the Way to Work

Marco was driving to work. He was going to drop his aunt, Adela, off at her friend's house, but they didn't get to their destinations.

Why didn't Marco and Adela get to their destinations?

To find out what happened, put the story in order.

_____ Next he swerved right to avoid hitting the other car and smashed into a tree instead.

_____ Meanwhile, the other driver drove off when the light changed, unaware that he had caused an accident.

__8__ Before the police officer finished talking to Marco and Adela, the tow truck arrived.

_____ As Marco was driving to work, a driver cut in front of him at an intersection.

_____ While one officer called for a tow truck, the other one recorded Marco's and Adela's statements about the accident.

_____ Then Marco slammed on the brakes, but they didn't hold.

_____ A police car arrived a few minutes after the other car left.

_____ Slowly they got out of the car. Although the car was damaged, they were unhurt.

A. Complete these sentences.

1. The brakes gave out because _____.

2. The dented fender can _____.

3. Repairing the brakes will cost _____.

4. The body work will cost _____.

5. Adela and Marco will _____.

6. Marco will have to pay at least _____.

B. Think and talk about the questions.

1. Have you ever had car trouble, such as an accident or a breakdown?
2. What happened?
3. Was anyone else involved?
4. How much did it cost?

The Bill

Parts/Materials:

rotors & brake pads	$175
4 qts. oil	$ 12
r/f fender	$125
cl. coat paint	$ 68
tint	$ 10
Subtotal	**$390**

OTHER SERVICES

Towing service	$ 37
Pickup charge	$ —
Cleaning	$ 10
Tolls	$ 2
Subtotal	**$ 49**

S & J Garage

Insurance Co.: _National_

Owner: _Marco Silva_   Date: _Nov. 12, 2005_

Year	Make	Model	Odometer	Registration No.
1990	Ford	Tempo	78,045	893-050 CF

Work to Be Done	Hours	Labor (@ $30/hour)
rotors & brake pads	3.9	$ 117
oil change	.5	$ 15
replace r/f fender	6.3	$189
clear coat / paint fender	2.0	$ 60
tint to match		
	$ 381

TOTAL SERVICE

Labor	12.7 hrs. @ $30/hr.	$ 381
Parts/Materials		$ 390
Other services		$ 49
	Subtotal $ —
	TOTAL $ 820

A. Answer the questions.

1. What items on this bill seem wrong?
2. What would you say to the mechanic about the errors or additions?

 B. Write the answers.

Cross out or make changes on the bill.
What should the total cost really be? _____

Work with a partner.
One person uses Form A.
The other uses Form B.

Marco and Adela are working on
Marco's car. They need to change
the oil and the transmission fluid.

You are Marco.
Your partner is Adela.

Adela is helping Marco change
the oil. Marco has some questions.

A. Ask your partner for instructions.

1. Ask how often you should
   change the oil.
2. Ask what tools you need
   to do the job.
3. Ask when the best time is to drain the oil.
4. Ask how you loosen the drain plug.
5. Ask what you use the wrench for.

Now Adela is changing the transmission fluid. She isn't sure how to
do it and has some questions. She asks Marco to find the information
in the automobile repair manual.

B. Find the information for your partner in the steps below.
   (Note: The steps are not in the correct order.)

a. Shift the car to neutral or park and put on the parking brake.
b. Do not overfill the transmission fluid. Overfilling causes severe problems.
c. Check that the transmission fluid is red.
d. The car should be parked with the engine on.
e. Check the fluid when the transmission is hot.
f. The fluid level should be between the second and third notches.

Maintaining a Car: Form B

Work with a partner.
One person uses Form A.
The other uses Form B.

Marco and Adela are working on Marco's car. They need to change the oil and the transmission fluid.

You are Adela.
Your partner is Marco.

Adela is helping Marco change the oil. Marco has some questions.

A. Find the information for your partner in the steps below.

(Note: The steps are not in the correct order.)

a. Change the oil only when the engine is at the normal operating temperature.

b. Change the oil every 4,000 miles or every six months.

c. Remove the oil filter with the wrench and empty the oil into the drain pan.

d. Use the jack to hoist up the car.

e. You need a wrench, a drain pan for used oil, and a jack.

f. Turn the drain plug to the left by hand.

Now Adela is changing the transmission fluid. She isn't sure how to do it and has some questions. She asks Marco to find the information in the automobile repair manual.

B. Ask your partner for instructions.

1. Ask when to check the fluid.
2. Ask whether the car should be turned on or off.
3. Ask what gear the car should be in.
4. Ask what notch the fluid level should be on the dipstick.
5. Ask if it's OK to overfill the transmission fluid.

After his accident, Marco went home and read his insurance policy.

National Insurance Company

Policy No.: L 912001-76
Name of Insured: Marco Silva
Auto No. 1: 1990 Ford Tempo

Discounts: None
Surcharge: None
Quarterly payment: $348.75

Coverage

Property Damage Liability:	$50,000 per claim
Bodily Injury Liability:	$25,000 per individual
Uninsured Motorist:	$500 deductible
Comprehensive:	No coverage
Collision:	$250 deductible
Towing:	No coverage

A. Match these words and their meanings.

1. towing
2. comprehensive
3. liability
4. deductible
5. coverage
6. collision

a. insurance that covers many things, including fire, theft, bad weather, and vandalism
b. an obligation to pay
c. the amount that you must pay before your insurance begins paying
d. insurance that covers damage to your car from hitting or being hit by another object or vehicle
e. having a car moved by another vehicle
f. what your insurance company will pay for

B. Write the answers.

1. What is not covered by Marco's insurance? _____

_____

2. How much does Marco have to pay a year for his insurance policy?

_____

Buying a Van

Stan wants to trade in his sports car for a van. Although he loves his car, he thinks a van would be more practical. He did some research at the library to find out more about vans.

The ASTROCHIEF (list price: $21,550) starts and runs well, but it only gets 17 mpg— low even for a van. A five-speed manual transmission is standard. Its four-speed automatic transmission ($750) shifted smoothly when test-driven. **BRAKES** continue to be decent, although stopping distances are still a bit long. **ROUTINE HANDLING** is clumsier than in earlier models, and this AstroChief is slow to respond in emergencies. There's no improvement in the ride of the new model. It remains hard and noisy. **AIR BAGS** have been standard since the 2002 model. **AIR CONDITIONING** is a modest $420. **THE CARGO AREA** is enlarged, but it takes two people to remove the back bench (89 lbs.).

The TURBOMASTER (list price: $22,357) starts easily and runs well. An overall 20 mpg is a great improvement over last year's model. A three-speed automatic transmission is standard. Manual transmission is no longer available. **ROUTINE HANDLING** is satisfactory, but emergency handling is still clumsy on hard turns. **A NEW PACKAGE ($1,250)** will include antilock brakes and air bags (both highly recommended) and air conditioning. If purchased separately, these three items would set you back $2,228. **BRAKES** are firm and quick. Even without a full load, the ride is comfortable. **CARGO AREA** is excellent, but removing the 100-pound rear seat is a tough job.

A. Evaluate the vans.

List the pros and cons for each van.

	AstroChief	TurboMaster
Pros		
Cons		

B. Think and talk about the questions.

1. Which van would you choose?
2. Which features would make you choose one van over the other?

Stan decided that a new van would cost more than he could afford, so he decided to get a used model. Before he talked to the different dealers, he compared their ads. Each ad had different information, so he had many questions.

Write down the questions *you* would want answered.

One question for each ad is already written for you.

1

Guaranteed Lowest Prices

'02 AstroChiefs—loaded, a/c, mint cond, antilock brakes, air bag, AM/FM stereo

Up to **$2,200 matching down payment**

Sale Price: $16,390
Cash or Trade: .... −2,200
Dealer's Match: .... −2,200
YOUR PRICE: .... $ 11,990
10.9%   (only $249/mo.)

2

THIS YEAR'S ASTROCHIEF

Demo./ loaded, special 4K discount, under warranty

Original Price:.......... $21,225
Factory rebate: .... −1,500
Dealer rebate: .... −2,500
                         $17,225

Questions for Ad 1.

1. Who pays the $2,200 for "Cash or Trade?"
2. _____
3. _____
4. _____

Questions for Ad 2.

1. What does "loaded" mean?
2. _____
3. _____
4. _____

3

'98 TURBOMASTER VAN

black and silver, auto, AM/FM stereo, V-6, sunrf, exc. cond, eng. reblt in '01. New tires
$12,750 or BO

4

FREE cellular phone with every new van purchased this week!
'02 TURBOMASTER auto, lo miles, antilock brakes, a/c, cassette, factory warranty, former rental.

$16,441

Questions for Ad 3.

1. How many miles does it have on it?
2. _____
3. _____
4. _____

Questions for Ad 4.

1. How long does the warranty run?
2. _____
3. _____
4. _____

Getting a Car Loan

Stan called several places to get information on car loans.

A. Listen to the three conversations and take notes.

Each bank offers one incentive (a special feature or plan), which is better than the others.

Underline the three incentives in your notes.

	1. Herndon Savings Bank	2. Metropolitan Credit Union	3. Simmons Trust
Rates			
Down payment			
Length of loan			
Monthly costs			

B. Check (✔) the answer.

Which bank . . .

	1.	2.	3.
1. offers the best rate?			
2. will finance a maximum of 80% of the car's cost?			
3. gives regular customers a better rate?			
4. offers the least flexible financing?			
5. has the most impersonal service?			
6. will finance a maximum of 90% of the car's cost?			

C. Think and talk about the questions.

1. Which bank do you think Stan went to? Why?
2. Why does it pay to shop around for loans?

Marco has been taking evening classes. His English class was given a writing assignment. The topic is "Having a . . . Is a Big Financial Responsibility." Marco chose to write about the thing that has been most on his mind lately. His essay, "Having a Car Is a Big Financial Responsibility," got an A–.

Write a story about the expenses and responsibilities of owning a car.
The following list of possible costs should help.

purchase price	maintenance
interest on loan	repairs
registration fees	garage rental
taxes	gasoline
insurance	parking fees

_____

_____

_____

_____

_____

_____

_____

_____

_____

_____

_____

_____

_____

> Marco **was going** to school.
> Adela **wasn't driving** this morning.
> They **were talking** about the weather.
> They **weren't watching** for other drivers.

Complete this conversation between Adela and her friend Keiko.

1. Keiko: What happened? When I called this morning, you _____ (leave) the house.

2. Adela: While Marco _____ (drive), another car cut him off.

3. He slammed on the brakes, but they _____ (not hold).

4. Next thing we knew, we _____ (head) for a tree!

    Keiko: How awful! What happened to the other driver?

5. Adela: Nothing! While we _____ (sit) there, stunned, he drove off without a scratch!

6. Keiko: Did he know that he _____ (leave) the scene of an accident?

7. Adela: I don't think so. He _____ (not pay) attention.

> Marco's car hit a tree **because the brakes weren't holding.**
> **Because the brakes weren't holding,** Marco's car hit a tree.

Underline the reason clause in each sentence.

1. It's important to change a car's oil regularly so that the engine stays clean.
2. Marco tries to change his oil every 3,000 miles because his car is old.
3. Because he wants to save money, he usually changes the oil himself.
4. He always checks his equipment so he can do the oil change safely.
5. His car runs well because he takes good care of it.
6. Because he can't afford a new car, he wants his old car to last.

Wh- Questions: Past Tense

Who	was	a good driver?
	had	a good driving record?
When Where Why How	did	he get that car?

SAFE DRIVER INSURANCE PLAN

Driver	Description	Value
Wolanski, Gregor age: 48	**Safe driver credits on January 1** **Deductions:** NONE **Safe driver credits on December 31**	15 0 15
Wolanski, Ana age: 44	**Safe driver credits on January 1** **Deductions:** SPEEDING TICKET/ Wash, DC: 11-08 **Safe driver credits on December 31**	15 - 2 13
Wolanski, Stanislav age: 24	**Safe driver credits on January 1** **Deductions:** Major accident/ Herndon, VA: 03-15 **Safe driver credits on December 31**	15 - 4 11

Write a question for each answer. Use the past tense.

Question	Answer
Example: ___Who was the safest driver?___	Gregor.
1. _____	By being a good driver.
2. _____	Ana and Stan.
3. _____	Because she got a speeding ticket.
4. _____	In the fall.
5. _____	In Washington, D.C.
6. _____	He was in a major accident.
7. _____	Near his house.
8. _____	On March 15.

1 2 3 4 5 6 7 8 9 10 11 12
Under the Law ■ ■ ■ ■ ■ ■ ■ ■ ■

Questioned by the Police

What do you think happened to Quang?

What is the police officer doing?

Do you think the police officer will be able to help Quang? Why or why not?

A Mugging

Quang Tran came home late from work. When he got off the bus, he was thinking about his dinner. Suddenly a man jumped out and poked something hard in Quang's back.

The man spoke in a deep, raspy voice: "Don't make a sound. I have a gun. Give me your wallet and your jewelry. Quick."

Quang stayed calm. He knew that resisting was foolish. "OK. I'm not going to try anything. My wallet is in my back pocket. I'm reaching in to get it. Here it . . ." The man interrupted, "Shut up and move fast. Give me your watch and your rings." As the man spoke, Quang smelled cigarette smoke.

Quang slipped the watch off his wrist and passed it backward. Then he held up his hands so the mugger could see he wasn't wearing a ring. "I don't have any rings."

"Bah! Shut up! Don't turn around!" The mugger gave Quang a powerful shove. Quang lost his balance, fell, and banged his head on the pavement. The mugger took off. Quang could hear the man running down the street because his shoes made so much noise.

Quang started shouting, "Help! I've been mugged!" A neighbor came to his aid.

Write the answers.

1. Why didn't Quang notice the mugger? _____

   _____

2. What did the mugger want from Quang? _____

3. How did the mugger try to scare Quang? _____

   _____

4. How did Quang hit his head? _____

   _____

5. What did Quang notice about the mugger? _____

   _____

What Did You See?

The police officer asked Quang many different questions, because he was trying to get a description of the mugger.

A. Write a possible question for each answer.

1. _____? He was about my height.

2. _____? I don't remember, but he had a raspy voice.

3. _____? No, he was alone.

4. _____? I couldn't see, but when he ran, it sounded like he was wearing boots.

5. _____? He was very young, maybe 18 or 19.

6. _____? I could smell cigarette smoke.

B. How observant are you? Fill in the chart below.

Describe the person sitting behind you or next to you.
Do not look at the person you are describing.

height: _____	hair color: _____
weight: _____	eye color: _____
sex: _____	skin color: _____
age: _____	clothing: _____
other: _____	

POLICE BEAT:

Mugger Hits Herndon

During the week of December 2, the Herndon Police Department received reports of 12 muggings, out of a total of 44 logged calls. Police also listed a purse snatching, made 15 arrests, responded to 13 accidents, and answered 3 calls of vandalism.

Herndon Police Chief Edward Dowd suggests that all citizens of Herndon follow some simple guide-lines to avoid being mugged on the street. "Every citizen has a role to play in crime prevention," he asserted. "There are sensible precautions that everyone can take to be safer on the street."

Street robberies are a quick way for a criminal to make money. Muggers are always looking for an easy target. Common sense can help you avoid being the next victim.

- Be aware of your surroundings and stay in well-lighted areas at night. Muggers always prefer shadows.
- Stay with a crowd. There's safety in numbers.
- Hold your bag or purse close to your body to make it hard to snatch. Keep your wallet in a pocket, not in your bag or purse.
- Don't carry large sums of cash.
- Notify the police of strangers who are hanging around your home or apartment for no apparent reason, especially at night.
- Lock your car doors when driving your vehicle and whenever you leave it, no matter for how short a time.

Think and talk about the questions.

1. Have you or someone you know been a victim of a street crime? What happened?
2. Do you think the ideas for avoiding muggings are sensible ones?
3. What other precautions do you use to protect yourself?
4. What precautions do you take to avoid burglaries at your home?
5. Why do you have to take special precautions when you go on vacation?
6. What else can be done to prevent street crime?

Harassed by the Boss

Diep's supervisor, Joan Morris, works for Dr. Landers. Dr. Landers has been bothering Joan for a long time. She's told him many times that she doesn't like being touched or cornered. She doesn't like him to tell her she's beautiful and smells nice. He just laughs and says she should be grateful for the compliment. She gets upset and angry, but she's been afraid to do anything because she needs her job. She's been afraid she'll get a bad evaluation from him if she complains to the hospital. Joan is also afraid that everyone at work thinks she doesn't mind or that she encourages his attention. She's worried that people won't believe that she's being harassed.

Lately Joan has noticed that Dr. Landers has been harassing female student nurses, too. Joan can't ignore Dr. Landers any longer. She's going to file a complaint with the Equal Employment Opportunity Commission (EEOC).

A. Write your answers.

1. Why did Joan Morris wait so long to file a complaint about Dr. Landers?

   _____

2. What finally made her decide to file the complaint?

   _____

B. Think and talk about the questions.

1. Why do you think Dr. Landers keeps bothering Joan Morris even though she's asked him to stop?
2. How do you think she feels?
3. Why is it so hard for Joan to make him stop?
4. Have you ever had a problem with someone giving you attention you didn't want? Who was involved? What did you do?

E.E.O.C. Regulations

A. Check (✔) True or False.

	True	False
1. Sexual harassment always includes physical contact.		
2. A supervisor is guilty of sexual harassment only if he or she threatens to fire a subordinate.		
3. Sexual harassment includes any kind of unwanted physical contact.		
4. Not many women workers say that they've been sexually harassed.		
5. Workers who are sexually harassed don't always do their best work.		
6. It's considered harassment if a supervisor pressures an employee for a date.		

B. Think and talk about the questions.

1. Do you agree with the EEOC definition of sexual harassment?
2. What do people think about sexual harassment in your native country?

A Family Fight

Three friends have been comparing stories about their week. Diep talked about Quang's mugging and her supervisor's problem at work.

Roberto talked about his son, Eddy, who thought he had won a free trip to Florida.

Yolette told her friends about a sad event that happened to her neighbor. Last night Al called the police because their neighbor, Marty Evans, was beating up his wife, Sara.

"We heard terrible noises and yelling. When the police got there, Marty didn't want to let them in. He said they couldn't enter his apartment without his permission or without a warrant. Marty wouldn't cooperate with the police. Finally Sara managed to step out in the hall to talk with the police. She was crying because Marty had broken her arm. The police took her to the hospital. I hope she's going to be all right," Yolette said.

Diep, Roberto, and Yolette discussed what happens in their native countries when husbands beat wives or parents beat children. They agreed that some ideas and laws in this country are different from those in other countries.

Think and talk about the questions.

1. Did Al and Yolette do the right thing?
2. What else could they have done?
3. How do you think Sara feels? How do you think Marty feels?
4. What would you have done if you were Al or Yolette?
5. Do you think it is all right for men to beat women?
6. Do you think it is all right for parents to beat children?

After Sara Evans was released from the hospital, the police took her to a shelter for battered women. A volunteer worker told Sara that it was against the law for Marty to beat her. The volunteer also said that it's very hard for violent husbands to stop. Sara knew the woman was right and decided to press charges. The police went to Sara's apartment with an arrest warrant for Marty.

MIRANDA RIGHTS

In 1966, the Supreme Court of the United States decided that police officers had to follow certain procedures when interrogating someone accused of a crime. Miranda rights protect people against forced confessions. According to the Miranda decision, criminal suspects must be told the following:

1. they do not *have* to answer a police officer's questions until their attorney is present;
2. they have the right to hire an attorney to defend them; and
3. if they can't afford to pay, the court will assign an attorney to defend them for free.

Find the word or phrase that means the same as . . .

1. lawyer: _____

2. asking questions: _____

3. blamed: _____

4. protect or help: _____

5. steps or actions: _____

6. be able to pay for: _____

7. employ: _____

Watch Out: Deceptive Advertising

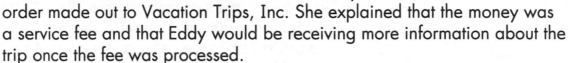

Roberto told his friends at school about an incident that happened to his son, Eddy. Eddy received a postcard in the mail that said that he and his family had won a free trip to Florida. The postcard was from a company called Vacation Trips, Inc.

Eddy was very excited. He knew that his family would be so pleased that he had won this fabulous vacation. The card instructed Eddy to call a special 800 number in order to claim his prize. He called the number and spoke to a woman who asked him to send a $20 money order made out to Vacation Trips, Inc. She explained that the money was a service fee and that Eddy would be receiving more information about the trip once the fee was processed.

Eddy took $20 from his savings, purchased the money order, and mailed it. Weeks went by and Eddy didn't hear anything more about the free vacation. Finally he told his father what had happened. Roberto realized that Eddy had been tricked.

Eddy was disappointed and angry that he hadn't really won a Florida vacation. But he learned a lesson from the experience.

A. What happened? List each thing Eddy did in the story.

1. _Eddy received a postcard that said he and his family had won a free trip to Florida._

2. _____

3. _____

4. _____

5. _____

B. Think and talk about the questions.

1. Why do you think Eddy responded to the postcard in this way?
2. Could Roberto have done anything to help his son?
3. Have you ever been told that you had won a big prize? If so, did you believe it?
4. How can you avoid problems like this?

Do you practice sensible safety precautions on the street, at work, in your car, and in your home? Take this quick quiz and judge for yourself. Get all seven right and you're being safety smart! A score of five or six means you're in good shape. Lower than five means you'd better watch out!

CHOOSE THE CORRECT SENTENCE IN EACH PAIR.

1. ___ A. If a mugger appears to have a weapon, scream for help.
   ___ B. If a mugger appears to have a weapon, don't panic or resist.

2. ___ A. Keep your car doors locked when you're driving your car.
   ___ B. Keep your car doors unlocked so you can jump out in an emergency.

3. ___ A. Let bushes and trees near your house grow so no one can see in.
   ___ B. Keep bushes and trees near your house trimmed so robbers can't hide behind them.

4. ___ A. Picking up hitchhikers is a nice thing to do, especially in bad weather.
   ___ B. Picking up hitchhikers is a foolish and risky thing to do.

5. ___ A. If a stranger needs to use your phone, make him or her wait outside while you make the call for him or her.
   ___ B. If a stranger needs to use your phone, it's usually OK if he or she offers to pay for the call.

6. ___ A. In this country, police can enter a house without the permission of the owner only with a legal search warrant.
   ___ B. In this country, police can enter a house at any time without the permission of the owner.

7. ___ A. If your neighborhood is safe, you don't need to lock your doors during the day.
   ___ B. You should keep your doors locked at all times, no matter where you live.

Answers: 1-B, 2-A, 3-B, 4-B, 5-A, 6-A, 7-B

After Quang was mugged, Diep became very concerned about her safety and the safety of her family and friends. She didn't want others to be victims of a crime like Quang had been. Diep decided to tell her brother's story in the hospital newsletter.

> *An Open Letter to My City Hospital Co-Workers:*
>
> *Some of you may have heard that my brother, Quang Tran, was mugged last week on Highland Street, right near the hospital. The street was dark and no one was around, so it was the perfect spot for a crime. Fortunately, Quang only received minor cuts and bruises, but the mugger took his wallet and watch.*
>
> *This experience has been very disturbing for our entire family. I think that it's about time that we voiced our opinions about the lack of safety in this neighborhood. We need more lights on the streets, and we also need more police officers in the area.*
>
> *Anyone interested in forming a committee to help make our streets safer, please call me at extension 2471.*
>
> *Sincerely,*
> *Diep Tran*

Write a short article for a newsletter.

Possible subjects include:
- safety or unsanitary conditions in your neighborhood, school, or workplace
- building or street maintenance
- communication with the police

Be sure to mention why you are interested in the subject. If you write about a current problem, try to convince others to help you correct the situation.

_____

_____

_____

_____

_____

_____

Have Haven't	I you we they	asked for help?	Yes,	I you we they	have. haven't.
Has Hasn't	he she it		No,	he she it	has. hasn't.

Complete this conversation between Ms. Hays and Kate, a student nurse. Use *have/has* or *haven't/hasn't*.

1. Ms. Hays: _____ Dr. Landers bothered you before today?

2. Kate: Yes, he _____. Several times. _____ anyone else complained?

3. Ms. Hays: Yes. Others have. _____ you talked to your supervisor?

4. Kate: Yes, I have. _____ Charlie spoken to you?

5. Ms. Hays: No, he _____. _____ you written down what happened?

6. Kate: No, I _____. I'm afraid I'll get in trouble.

7. Ms. Hays: You won't get in any trouble for reporting harassment.

Active	Passive
A student filed a harassment report.	A harassment report was filed.

Rewrite the sentences in the passive form.

1. A man poked something hard in Quang's back.

   _____

2. The man grabbed Quang's wallet and watch.

   _____

3. Quang heard the sounds of footsteps running away.

   _____

Who	**filed**	a report?

What		**filed?**
When Where Why	**was/were**	it/they **filed?**

How		it **get filed?**
What	**did**	it **say?**

Read the story on page 122. Then write questions for these answers.

Question	Answer
_____	Eddy did.
_____	He thought he'd won a vacation.
_____	In Florida.
_____	A woman at Vacation Trips, Inc.
_____	Weeks after he sent the money order.
_____	Because he really didn't win a prize.
_____	By cheating people.
_____	To be very careful about "free offers."

Prepositions of Time	Prepositions of Place
Yolette had questions <u>before</u> class.	She sat <u>close to</u> the door.
She raised her hand <u>during</u> class.	She was <u>in</u> the front row.
Her question was answered <u>after</u> the demonstration.	She sat <u>with</u> some friends.

Complete each sentence with an appropriate preposition.

1. Light the hallway _____ the night.

2. Stay _____ well-lighted places.

3. Walk _____ other people whenever possible.

4. Keep your purse or bag _____ your side.

5. Don't let strangers enter an empty hallway _____ you.

6. Check the backseat of your car _____ getting in.

1 2 3 4 5 6 7 8 9 10 11 12

Can I Buy a House? ■ ■ ■ ■ ■ ■ ■ ■

For Sale

What are Al and Yolette doing?
What are they talking about?

Which is Better for You?

TO BUY OR TO RENT?
That Is the Question.

Many people thinking about the purchase of a house wonder whether it's better to rent or to buy. Down payments, mortgage and interest costs, regular maintenance, and unexpected expenses sometimes scare off potential home owners. According to Marsha Decter, president of Decter Real Estate in Herndon, "Buying a home is the major investment of most people's lives. Traditionally, it's the American dream." But is it right for everyone? And what are the benefits of renting? Let's look at some of the facts:

	RENTER	OWNER
TAX ADVANTAGES	You have no deductions or very limited state deductions.	You can deduct all mortgage interest on your federal tax return.
LONG-TERM INVESTMENT VALUE	You have no investment value.	Your investment value is usually very good.
MAINTENANCE RESPONSIBILITY	You are usually not responsible at all or have very limited responsibility.	You are fully responsible for all maintenance.
EMERGENCY PROBLEMS	You usually have very limited responsibility when problems occur.	You are fully responsible for all problems.
IMPROVEMENTS	You need your landlord's approval. You may have to pay or share cost. Improvements remain with property.	You make improvements at your own discretion. You pay full cost. Improvements may add value to your investment.

Think and talk about the questions.

1. What are some other advantages of renting and owning? What are some other disadvantages?
2. In your native country, did you own or rent your home?
3. If you rent, do you plan to buy a home someday? If so, what kind of home would you like?

Al and Yolette want to buy a house. After talking to several real estate agents, the Jamisons found an agent they liked. She listened to them and gave them the information they needed about buying a house. The agent also asked Al and Yolette a lot of questions so that she knew what they wanted in a house. Here's an information sheet she gave them, which describes one house.

 Underline the items in this information sheet that Al and Yolette want in a house.

DECTER REAL ESTATE
93 Union Street
Herndon, VA 22070
(703) 965-2033

RESIDENTIAL PROPERTY INFORMATION

Address:	75 Park Road, Manassas, VA
Near:	Central Ave.
Lot size:	6,200 sq. ft.
Assessment:	$78,800
Taxes:	$ 1,532

Asking price: $92,900

Type:	1-level ranch	Garage:	one car, attached
Exterior:	vinyl siding	Bsmt.:	full, unfinished
Roof:	asphalt shingle	Heat:	oil, tank
Appliances:	stove, dishwasher, refrig.	Amenities:	dining room, attic

	LR	DR	KT	BR1	BR2	BR3	BR4	BTHS	OTH
1st level	X	X	X	X	X			1 $1/2$	

REMARKS: A perfect starter home. Freshly painted ranch on quiet side street. New kitchen overlooking sunny yard. Lg. master bedroom w/ walk-in closet. Expandable attic/basement. Near public transportation.

Answer the questions.

1. What two things do they say they will consider in a house?
2. What questions do you think they still might have about this house?

Can We Get a Mortgage?

Al and Yolette are buying a house for $86,500. They made a 7.5% down payment and applied for an $80,000 mortgage. Their combined annual income before taxes and deductions is $34,865. A chart from the bank showed them that they easily qualify for an $80,000 mortgage at the current rate of 9%.

Income Needed to Qualify for a Mortgage

Loan Amount	$50,000	$75,000	$100,000
Interest Rate	Income Needed*		
8%	$15,724	$23,568	$31,447
9%	$17,242	$25,863	$34,484
10%	$18,085	$28,208	$37,611

*30-year loans; monthly payments (principal and interest) cannot exceed 28% of gross income.
Source: National Association of Realtors

A. Answer the questions.

1. What is the largest mortgage amount that Al and Yolette can borrow at 9%?
2. Why do you think banks and mortgage companies assume that people spend 28% of their income on mortgage payments?

Another chart showed Al and Yolette what their monthly payments will be.

Mortgage Payment Table at Various Interest Rates

Amount Borrowed	8%	9%	10%
	Monthly Payments* (principal + interest)		
$ 40,000	$294	$322	$351
$ 60,000	$440	$483	$527
$ 80,000	$587	$644	$702
$100,000	$734	$805	$878

* rounded off to nearest whole dollar *Source:* Federal Trade Commission

B. Answer the questions.

1. How much would monthly payments be on a $60,000 mortgage at 8%? 9%? 10%?
2. How would you figure monthly payments for a $90,000 mortgage at 9%?

What Will It Cost?

Al and Yolette had an inspector look at the house they planned to buy. They wanted to know if the house had any major problems and, if so, how much the repairs would cost. They also wanted to find out what some remodeling projects would cost. The inspector gave Al and Yolette this chart. They studied the information and decided to purchase the house.

Inspection Report
Property: 75 Park Road, Manassas, VA

Item	Condition/ Comments	Unit of Measure	Average Cost/unit
Replace roof with asphalt shingles	within 5 yrs.	sq. ft.	$ 1.50
Install new gutters and downspouts	1 yr.	foot	$ 1.75
Install new boiler	satisfactory	each	$ 3,150.00
Run electric line for dryer/range	satisfactory	each	$ 225.00
Install new storm windows	now	each	$ 115.00
Insulate attic	now	sq. ft.	$ .90
Remodel kitchen	optional	each	$ 10,500.00
Remodel bath	optional	each	$ 6,250.00
Add full bath	optional	each	$ 7,000.00

A. Answer the questions.

1. What things do Al and Yolette have to do to put the house in good condition? _____

_____

2. What things could they do if they wanted to improve the value of the house?

_____

B. Calculate the cost.

Al and Yolette decided to make the following improvements in their new home. Calculate the average cost of each and then the total cost.

1. insulation in attic floor, 18' x 30' $ _____

2. 12 storm windows $ _____

3. new gutters and downspouts in rear of house, 30' $ _____

4. Total $ _____

Thinking about a Move

A. Check (✔) True or False.

	True	False
1. Yolette and Al bought a house in Herndon.		
2. Their new house is near public transportation.		
3. Diep shares a bedroom with her children.		
4. Housing grants are for people who are working.		
5. Marco is working part-time now.		
6. Roberto wants to move.		
7. Stan has been looking for a roommate.		

B. Think and talk about the questions.

1. Would you like to move?
2. Where would you like to move? Why?
3. Where can you find out about housing grants in your community?

The Housing Grants Program provides housing subsidies to eligible needy persons who own or rent their home. The following are questions commonly asked about this program.

Q. Who may apply?
A. County residents who are 55 years or older or working families with at least one child under 18.

Q. What are the income limits?
A. Maximum gross income limits from all sources are:

Household Size	Income Limit	Household Size	Income Limit
1	$18,799	5	$29,534
2	$21,534	6	$33,000
3	$24,498	7	$34,889
4	$26,877	8 or more	$38,000

Q. How much will I receive from the Housing Grants Program?
A. Each household must pay a minimum of 30% of its gross income for rent or mortgage. Above that amount, the maximum housing grant you may receive is:
• up to $676 per month for working-family households (2–4 persons)
• up to $848 per month for working-family households (5 or more persons)
Your Housing Grant may never exceed 70% of your rent or mortgage.

Are they eligible?

Read the descriptions of these housing grant applicants.
Write whether they are eligible or not for a housing grant.
If they are ineligible, write the reason why.

1. a couple, with two small children, who make a combined income of $25,900

   _____

2. a 66-year-old man and his 58-year-old wife, who get a pension of $18,000, dividends of $8,490, and interest of $2,098 _____

3. a 42-year-old veteran, whose annual salary is $23,575, and her five children

   _____

4. a single father, with a 10-year-old daughter and 6-year-old son, who makes $2,100 a month _____

5. a family of five, with a monthly income of $2,600 _____

   _____

Choose a Roommate with Care

LIVING WITH A ROOMMATE

Once upon a time, roommates were people you lived with in college dormitories. Nowadays, living with a roommate is a growing trend for many young (and not-so-young) adults. Almost 5% of adults polled during the 1990 census reported living with roommates (nonromantic attachments), up from a little over 3.5% 10 years earlier and almost triple 1970's figures of about 1.5%. A major reason for this increase in roommate situations is economic: Rents, utility costs, and food prices have far outpaced the rise in individual income, so people are learning to share their living space along with their expenses.

A growing number of people are relying on bulletin boards or roommate-matching services to find roommates. When you don't know the potential roommate well or at all, you need to be very choosy. Here are some useful recommendations from professional roommate screeners.

- Be honest about your expectations and needs. Ask about the other person's habits: late hours; sharing food, clothes or belongings; how to deal with overnight guests; dishwashing and bathroom-cleaning inclinations.

- Trust your instincts. If something tells you it won't work out, it probably won't.

- Check references of the other person (especially any previous living arrangement).

- Ask to see the lease so that you know the full amount of the rent.

- A written agreement with a trial period of two to six months will give both sides a chance to get to know each other before deciding on a longer commitment. Get the agreement in writing to protect yourself legally.

Write the answers.

1. Why were more people living with roommates in 1990 than 20 years earlier?

   _____

2. What kind of person would you pick if you were going to share your home?

   _____

3. What questions would you ask that person? _____

   _____

   _____

4. What would be the hardest thing for you about sharing your home?

   _____

Stan and Marco are talking about rooming together. They want to make sure they can get along, so they're asking each other lots of questions. Their answers are written below. Complete the missing questions.

1. *Stan:* "Why _do you want to move_ ?"
   Marco: "I need a quieter place to live. I love Eddy and Cruz, but they sure can make noise."

2. *Stan:* "How much _____ ?"
   Marco: "I can afford between $300 and $350 for my share."

3. *Stan:* "What if _____ ?"
   Marco: "My aunt and uncle will give me a short-term loan."

4. *Stan:* "Where _____ ?"
   Marco: "I'd prefer to stay in Herndon, but I'm willing to look at other towns too."

5. *Marco:* "What do _____ ?"
   Stan: "Most nights I'll be working or studying, but I'll still be able to play basketball on Tuesdays. And of course, I like to see my friends on weekends."

6. *Marco:* "Do you _____ ?"
   Stan: "No, I prefer to get up early and go for a run."

7. *Marco:* "Do you _____ ?"
   Stan: "Not much. Just spaghetti and meatballs, bacon and eggs, you know. I guess we'll have to learn. Or eat out a lot."

8. *Marco:* "Now, where _____ ?"
   Stan: "Well, let's take a look at the newspaper and see what apartments are available!"

Finding a Place

Stan and Marco decided to get an apartment together. They looked through the ads and found five apartments they were interested in. Listen to their telephone conversations with the landlords and take notes.

 Write the pros and cons of each apartment.

	PROS	CONS
1. **HERNDON** spac 4 rms, 6th fl, lrg terr, all mod, $730 htd. (848-9090)		
2. **HERNDON** immac. 2 BR, lt & airy, w/w, w/d, pkg. space (848-6759)		
3. **MERRIFIELD** 20 mins. to downtown, nr. X-town bus, nice 5-rm apt. in house, furn or unfurn, ht/hw incl., yd, no pets, $725 no fee (893-0707)		
4. **VIENNA** 1 and 2 BR, from $595 incl. util, walk to shops, call 965-8164		
5. **RESTON** 2 BR, bsmt. apt. sep. entr., pkg. avail. $565. Call for appt. 215-1105		

Write about your home here and in your native country.
The following questions may help you make comparisons.

Where did/do you live?

- in a city, a suburb, a town, the country?
- near water, in the mountains?
- in a house, an apartment?
- by yourself, with others?

What was/is your home like?

- big, small?
- rented, owned?

What did/do you like best/least about your homes?

_____

_____

_____

_____

_____

_____

> The <u>new</u> house is in Herndon. The rooms are <u>spacious</u>.
> All the windows have <u>insulated</u> glass. <u>Friendly</u> neighbors welcomed them.

Read this description of the Jamisons' new house. Underline the descriptive adjectives. On separate paper, write about your home. Use descriptive adjectives.

The house is on a single floor. You enter through a narrow hallway. On the right is an airy living room. It has a picture window that looks out on an attractive garden. On the left is a formal dining room. It has a corner cabinet for dishes. Behind the dining room is a sunny kitchen. There is a broom closet with a deep shelf. The stairs to the finished basement are in the kitchen, too. There are three bedrooms on the other side of the house. The master bedroom has generous closets, but needs a coat of fresh paint. The other bedrooms have worn wallpaper and modest closets.

<u>What</u> did the banker say <u>about</u> our mortgage? <u>What about</u> our mortgage?	The banker said that it has been approved.
<u>What</u> can we do <u>if</u> we don't get this house? <u>What if</u> we don't get this house?	She said that the approval can be transferred to another house.

Complete the conversation with *What . . . about* or *What . . . if.*

1. Stan: _____ did the landlord say _____ the apartment?

   Marco: He said that it's available. But it's expensive.

2. Stan: _____ we took an apartment on a lower floor?

   Marco: He said that 12A is the only one available on Green Street.

3. Stan: _____ trading the parking space for lower rent?

   Marco: I think that he'd consider that idea.

Regular		Irregular	
Adjective	*Comparative*	*Adjective*	*Comparative*
small	small<u>er</u>	roomy	room<u>ier (than)</u>
comfortable	<u>more</u> comfortable <u>(than)</u>	bad	worse

Stan and Marco need things for their new kitchen.
Here are two ads they can check out.

```
                    ...wivei locking      |                                    | Man...
  ...ed frame   wheels, great condition, Clean $75.  | RESTON—MOVING SALE        | Quilts, ...
  ...ash Only.                                 | Kitchen gear: sm. appliances: good to | China, ...
                YARD SALE IN HERNDON    | excel. condition: $15 each; self-  | Pictur...
  FOR SALE      Clean refrigerator: $100. small | cleaning stove: $75. Deluxe side-by- | Msic b...
  ...Cabinet; VCR;  appliances/ good condition: $10: | side refrig. still under warranty ($800 |
  ...s and garden   hairdryer, blender, automatic coffee | new) asking $350, freezer needs | HOUS...
  ...lassware   maker + box of pots, pans & utensils, | defrosting. Assorted pots/pans/ | Book S...
  ...ient   all fair condition: $35 for whole box. | flatware/dishes $50.          | Head...
                    GARAGE SALE
```

A. Complete the sentences with comparative forms.

Example: The sale in Reston is _____ *closer than* _____ (close) the one in Herndon.

1. The items are _____ (expensive).

2. But they seem to be in _____ (good) condition.

3. The refrigerator in Reston seems to be _____ (fancy), too.

4. But the one in Herndon is a lot _____ (cheap).

5. It seems to be _____ (clean), too.

6. They decide to check out the _____ (convenient) sale first.

B. Look at the ads. Then complete the sentences.

I'd buy the coffee pot from _____ because _____

_____

I'd buy the refrigerator from _____ because _____

_____

Verbs: Past and Present Participles

Verbs: Past and Present Participles

	Present Tense	Past Tense	Past Participle	Present Participle
Regular	turn	turned	turned	turning
	arrive	arrived	arrived	arriving
	stop	stopped	stopped	stopping
	study	studied	studied	studying
Irregular	be	was/were	been	being
	go	went	gone	going
	have	had	had	having
	find	found	found	finding
	take	took	taken	taking
	give	gave	given	giving

Complete the verb list.

	Present Tense	Past Tense	Past Participle	Present Participle
Regular	1. use			
	2. clean			
	3. start			
	4. plan			
	5. _____			
	6. _____			
	7. _____			
Irregular	1. see			
	2. think			
	3. speak			
	4. come			
	5. write			
	6. get			
	7. know			
	8. do			
	9. make			
	10. _____			
	11. _____			
	12. _____			
	13. _____			
	14. _____			

Past	Present Perfect
I **worked** there from 1995 to 2000.	I've **worked** here since 1995.
Al **went** to New York in March.	Al **has gone** to New York for a few days.
They **saw** the movie last week.	They **have seen** the movie three times.
We **had** a meeting last month.	We **haven't had** another meeting yet.
I **used** a computer in my last job.	**Have** you ever **used** a computer?

A. Stan is talking to Quang about moving. Underline the present perfect sentences.

1. *Stan:* "Marco and I have finally found an apartment that we both like."
2. *Quang:* "That's great. Have you signed the lease yet?"
3. *Stan:* "Yes. We met with the landlord yesterday."
4. *Quang:* "Are you going to move into the apartment soon?"
5. *Stan:* "In two weeks. I've waited a long time to get a place of my own."
6. *Quang:* "Have you started to pack yet?"
7. *Stan:* "Not really, but I've already gotten some boxes."
8. *Quang:* "Were you planning to rent a van or truck for the move?"
9. *Stan:* "No. We both have cars, so we're using them. We might have to take several trips, but that's not a big problem."

B. Joan Morris and Diep Tran are going over Diep's evaluation. Complete the sentences, using the present perfect.

1. *Diep:* "Good afternoon. I _____ (come) to talk about my evaluation."
2. *Joan:* "Yes. Have a seat please. I _____ (get) your evaluation back from the personnel office, so let's go over it together. Here's a copy for you."
3. *Diep:* "Thank you. I _____n't _____ (see) it yet."
4. *Joan:* "It shows that you _____ (be) a dependable member of our team."
5. *Diep:* "I think that I _____ (learn) a lot in the past year."
6. *Joan:* "_____ you _____ (think) about taking any business courses?"
7. *Diep:* "I _____ just _____ (complete) a computer course at the Community College. It's not mentioned on the form."
8. *Joan:* "Probably the personnel office _____n't _____ (receive) that information yet. Did you tell them about it?"
9. *Diep:* "No, I _____n't _____ (speak) to them yet."

Verbs: Passive Voice

Tense	Active	Passive
Present	The company **reuses** the paper. The teacher **assigns** the children to teams.	The paper **is reused**. The children **are assigned** to teams.
Past	Someone **stole** our car. Some thieves **took** our TV and VCR.	Our car **was stolen**. The TV and VCR **were taken**.
Present perfect	The landlord **has fixed** the sink.	The sink **has been fixed**.
Future	Someone **will repair** the roof. I am **going to clean** the bottles.	The roof **will be repaired**. The bottles **are going to be cleaned**.

The Silvas bought a house. There was a lot of work to do.

A. Underline the passive sentences.

1. The furniture was moved to the new house last weekend.
2. The kitchen appliances were hooked up on Saturday.
3. The kitchen hasn't been remodeled yet.
4. The seller added a new bathroom two years ago.
5. The gutters on the roof were replaced.
6. The Silvas repainted the bedrooms.

B. Help Adela complete a form for the realty company. Use the passive voice.

DECTER REAL ESTATE

We are taking a survey of our clients. Please tell us what was done to your house before you moved in and what will be done in the next two years.

Done

1. The bedrooms _____ _____. (paint)
2. The attic _____ _____. (insulate)
3. The living room carpet _____ _____. (clean)
4. The grass _____ _____. (cut)
5. New storm windows _____ _____. (install)

To Be Done

1. A family room _____ _____. (add)
2. Old wallpaper _____ _____. (remove)
3. A deck _____ _____. (build)
4. The kitchen cabinets _____ _____. (refinish)
5. The refrigerator _____ _____. (replace)

Eddy and Cruz **have been studying** about the environment at school.
They **haven't been working** on the same research projects.
The class **has been cleaning** up part of the river.
How long **has** the town council **been considering** the new proposal?
Why **has** MediKit **been looking** at Herndon as the site for its new factory?

Al is talking to the mechanic about his car.

A. Underline the sentences in the present perfect continuous tense.

1. *Mechanic:* "So what's wrong with your car?"

2. *Al:* "I've been noticing a strange clicking noise in the engine."

3. *Mechanic:* "How long have you been hearing this noise?"

4. *Al:* "It just started a couple of days ago. But I've also been having trouble starting the car."

5. *Mechanic:* "That could just be the battery. We'll check it out. Have any of the lights been blinking on the dashboard?"

6. *Al:* "No, that hasn't been a problem. But the car has been stalling a lot even after the motor has been running for a while."

B. Complete the sentences. Use the present perfect continuous tense.

1. *Mechanic:* "I _____ (work) on this car since 2:00. I think we got rid of the clicking sound. We put in a new belt."

   Al: "Is the motor still stalling when you start it?"

2. *Mechanic:* "No. It _____ (run) fine all afternoon—no stalling, no problem starting it."

   Al: "That's great."

3. *Mechanic:* "_____ you _____ (use) the car for long trips or just around town?"

   Al: "Both. We took a trip to Atlanta a few months ago."

4. *Mechanic:* "What kind of gas _____ you _____ (put) in your car?"

   Al: "I usually use premium."

5. *Mechanic:* "It looks like you _____ (take) good care of the car."

   Al: "I _____ (teach) my nephew Marco the basics, so he _____ (help) me with the maintenance."

Verbs: *"Unreal" Conditional*

> If I **were** rich, I would buy a house.
> If Marco **lost** his job, he would go back to school.
> If everyone **helped** us, the job would get done more quickly.
> If Roberto **didn't stay** out so late, he wouldn't be so tired.
> Where would you go if you **had** a vacation?
> Who would you talk to if you **heard** about a problem at work?

A. Match the parts of the sentences.

1. If there were more streetlights,
2. If we fixed up the vacant lot,
3. If we reported strangers hanging around,
4. More neighbors would help
5. Our children would be safer
6. Our street would look better

a. the police would stop and question them.
b. if we organized a Neighborhood Watch.
c. strangers wouldn't hang around.
d. if we planted some flowers.
e. the children could use it as a playground.
f. if we asked them.

B. Complete these sentences.

1. There would be less crime if _____.
2. People would be safer if _____.
3. If there were more police, _____.
4. If my child joined a gang, _____.
5. If I were attacked, _____.

C. Complete these wishes.

1. If I were President, _____.
2. If my English were better, _____.
3. I would cure all sick people if _____.
4. The world would be a better place if _____.

I You We They	**have** **haven't**	**had**	all the prerequisites.
He She It	**has** **hasn't**	**finished**	

Complete the sentences. Then write a sentence about a goal you have accomplished and one you haven't.

Example: Stan ____has accomplished____ (accomplish) some of his goals.

1. He _____ (take) two computer courses and

   _____ (get) good grades.

2. He _____ (carry) a full academic load so far.

3. But he _____ (not begin) the business sequence yet.

4. He and Marco _____ (find) a nice apartment.

5. They _____ (make) a lot of improvements in it, too.

6. Stan _____ (learn) new "people" skills this year.

7. So far he and Marco _____ (not have) any serious
   arguments.

8. He _____ (change) his attitude at work, too.

9. His boss thinks he _____ (become) a better worker.

I have _____

_____

I haven't _____

_____

TROUBLESHOOTING

Model JNF-1221 VCR

PROBLEM	POSSIBLE SOLUTION
VCR won't turn on.	1. Check the AC cord and outlet. 2. If the LOCK light is on, press and hold the DISPLAY button for 10 seconds until the LOCK light is off. 3. For further assistance, see Chapter 1, "Your New VCR."
VCR controls don't work.	1. To work safely, turn off the VCR before continuing. 2. Unplug the power cord for at least 2 minutes. Then plug the power cord back in and turn on the VCR. 3. If controls still don't work, see Chapter 1, "Your New VCR."
VCR does not record TV programs.	1. Check the VCR tuning. 2. If the input selection on the VCR reads "L," you must switch it to TUNER by pressing the INPUT button. 3. For additional information, see Chapter 2, "VCR Operations."

Complete the sentences with *can/can't, should/shouldn't,* or *must/mustn't.*

1. If your VCR won't turn on, you _____ check the AC cord and outlet first.

2. The VCR _____ be turned on if the LOCK light is on.

3. The DISPLAY button _____ be pressed down for at least 10 seconds.

4. If the VCR still won't turn on, you _____ read Chapter 1 for more help.

5. You _____ leave the VCR off when you are checking the controls.

6. You _____ unplug the power cord for two minutes if the controls don't work.

7. Your VCR _____ be set to "L" if you want to record programs.

8. To record programs, you _____ have the input selection on TUNER.

9. To switch to TUNER, you _____ press the INPUT button.

10. If you need more help, you _____ refer to the chapter indicated.

Who	**was/were**	insured?
When Where Why	**was** **were**	it effective? they covered?
How much		the premium/s?
How much What	**did**	it cost?

Policy for: Wolanski, Gregor; Wolanski, Ana; Wolanski, Stanislav
Effective: January 1, 2004 to December 31, 2004
Agent: Savemore Insurance Agency, Reston, VA

	Limits	Deductible (Amount you pay)	Premium (Costs)
Compulsory insurance			
Injury to others	$20,000 per person $40,000 per accident	None	$ 238.
Personal injury	$8,000 per person	None	$75.
Optional insurance			
Collision	Actual cash value	$500.	$536.
Comprehensive	Actual cash value	$500.	$102.

Write questions for the answers about the insurance policy.

Questions	Answer

Example: __What insurance is compulsory?__ Injury to others and personal injury.

1. _____ The Wolanski family.

2. _____ It ends on the last day of the year.

3. _____ Because collision costs are so high.

4. _____ In Reston, Virginia.

5. _____ It isn't required by law.

6. _____ The personal injury limit is $8,000 per person.

Cause		Effect
If Diep <u>makes</u> less than the limit,	<u>then</u> her children	<u>are/will be eligible</u> for free lunches. <u>can get</u> free school lunches. <u>will get</u> free school lunches.
If you <u>make</u> more than the limit,	<u>then</u> your child	<u>isn't /won't be eligible</u> for free lunches. <u>can't get</u> free school lunches. <u>won't get</u> free school lunches.

Application for Free School Lunches
You can apply for free school lunches for students in elementary through high school.
Your monthly income level must not exceed these limits.

Number in home	Monthly income limit	Number in home	Monthly income limit
2	$1735	5	$3076
3	2182	6	3523
4	2629	For each add'l family member add $448.	

Complete the *if/then* **sentences.**

Example: If a single parent has two sons and makes $1,500 a month, _____

_____ <u>then the boys are eligible for free school lunches.</u> _____

1. If a couple with four children have a yearly income of $18,000, _____

   _____

2. If a family with six children makes $5,000 a month, _____

   _____

3. If a grandmother raising her granddaughter has an income of $10,000, _____

   _____

4. If _____

   then all three elementary school girls will be able to get free school lunches.

5. If _____

   then my twins won't be eligible for free school lunches.

States and Their Standard Postal Abbreviations

Alabama	AL	Montana	MT
Alaska	AK	Nebraska	NE
Arizona	AZ	Nevada	NV
Arkansas	AR	New Hampshire	NH
California	CA	New Jersey	NJ
Colorado	CO	New Mexico	NM
Connecticut	CT	New York	NY
Delaware	DE	North Carolina	NC
Florida	FL	North Dakota	ND
Georgia	GA	Ohio	OH
Hawaii	HI	Oklahoma	OK
Idaho	ID	Oregon	OR
Illinois	IL	Pennsylvania	PA
Indiana	IN	Rhode Island	RI
Iowa	IA	South Carolina	SC
Kansas	KS	South Dakota	SD
Kentucky	KY	Tennessee	TN
Louisiana	LA	Texas	TX
Maine	ME	Utah	UT
Maryland	MD	Vermont	VT
Massachusetts	MA	Virginia	VA
Michigan	MI	Washington	WA
Minnesota	MN	West Virginia	WV
Mississippi	MS	Wisconsin	WI
Missouri	MO	Wyoming	WY

Other Postal Abbreviations

New York City	NYC	Puerto Rico	PR
Los Angeles	LA	United States	US
District of Columbia	DC	United States of America	USA

The United States of America

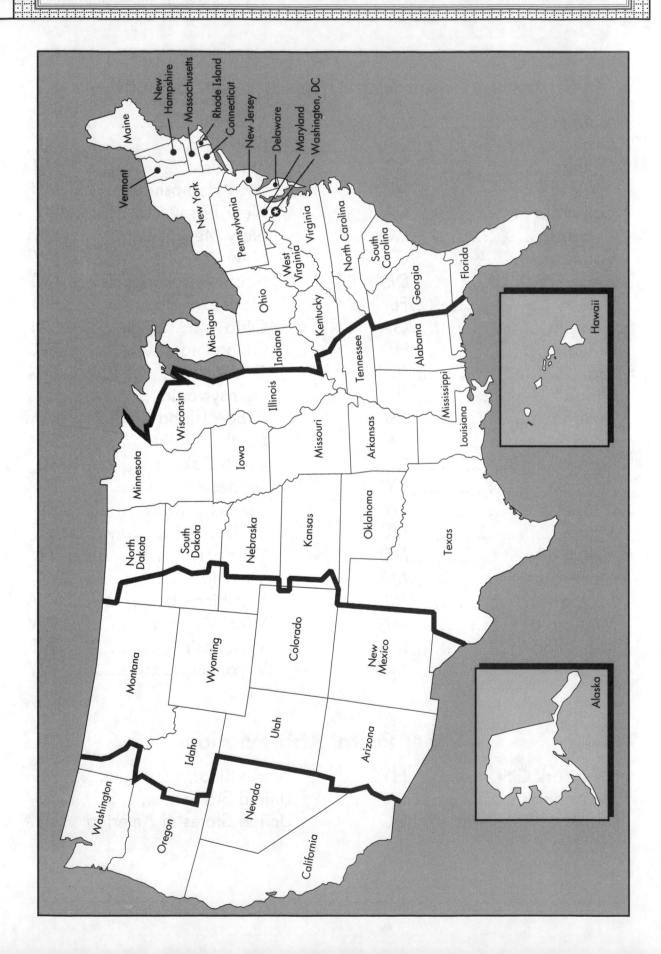

Common Abbreviations in Addresses

Avenue .... Ave.
Boulevard............... Blvd.
Drive .... Dr.
Lane .... Ln.
Place .... Pl.
Road .... Rd.
Square .... Sq.
Street..................... St.

Apartment .... Apt.
Room .... Rm.

Island .... Is./Isl.
Mount/Mountain ..... Mt.

Post Office .... PO

Directions

East...................... E
North .... N
South.................... S
West .... W

Northeast............... NE
Northwest .... NW
Southeast .... SE
Southwest.............. SW

Time Periods

second .... sec.
minute .... min.
hour .... hr.
week .... wk.
month .... mo.
year .... yr.

a.m./AM ... between midnight and noon
p.m./PM ... between noon and midnight

Days of the Week

Sunday .... Sun./Su
Monday .... Mon./M
Tuesday .... Tues./Tu
Wednesday .... Wed./W
Thursday .... Thurs./Thu./Th
Friday.................... Fri./F
Saturday .... Sat./S

Months

January.................. Jan.
February .... Feb.
March.................... Mar.
April...................... Apr.
May .... —
June .... Jun.
July .... Jul.
August .... Aug.
September.............. Sept.
October .... Oct.
November.............. Nov.
December .... Dec.

Personal Identification Terms

female .... F
male .... M

address .... addr.
middle initial .... m.i.
Social Security number ... Soc. Sec. no.
telephone number .... tel./tel. no.

152

Common Abbreviations and Symbols

Weights

gallon .... gal.
liter.......................... l.
ounce .... oz.
pound .... lb.
quart .... qt.

Measures

inch .... in.
foot .... ft.
yard .... yd.
mile .... mi.

square inch .... sq. in.
square foot .... sq. ft.
square yard .... sq. yd.
square mile .... sq. mi.

millimeter .... mm.
centimeter .... cm.
meter .... m.
kilometer .... km.

Common Symbols

and .... &
at/each .... @
degrees .... °
foot/feet .... '
inch/inches .... "
number .... #
or/per .... /
percent .... %

Academic Terms

credits .... cr.
department .... dept.
instructor .... instr.
section .... sec.

introduction .... intro.
advanced .... adv.

General Educational
Development .... GED
Associate of Arts .... A.A.
Bachelor of Arts .... B.A.
Bachelor of Science ...... B.S.
Master of Arts/Science .. M.A./S.
Doctor of Philosophy ...... Ph.D.

Other Common Abbreviations

annual percentage rate .. APR
arrive, arrival .... ar.
assistant .... asst.
company .... co.
including .... incl.
incorporated .... inc.
leave .... lv.
miles per gallon .... mpg
miles per hour .... mph
not applicable.............. N/A
number .... no.
television .... TV
videocassette recorder ... VCR
with .... w/